I0500213

Awesome Employee Playbook

25 Exercises and Tons of Tips

CÉLESTE GRIMARD

Copyright © 2017 Céleste Grimard, Canada

All rights reserved. All materials on these pages are copyrighted by Céleste Grimard. Reproduction, modification, storage of all or a part of this book in a retrieval system or retransmission, in any form or by any means, electronic, mechanical or otherwise is strictly prohibited without prior written permission from the author. Every effort has been made to indicate the sources of the material where available. If you are aware of sources of material for which references or citations are not provided, please contact us. This document does not constitute legal advice and is not a substitute for independent professional advice. This book was illustrated by Céleste Grimard.

ISBN-13: 978-1548083090

CreateSpace, Charleston, SC. USA

ACKNOWLEDGMENTS

I thank the hundreds of employees whose paths I crossed over the past decades. You have offered me priceless glimpses into the successes and challenges you encountered on your journeys toward becoming awesome employees. I've drawn from your inspiration in developing this compendium of exercises. I also thank Rhiannon Ward for her awesome assistance in editing and proofreading earlier drafts of this book.

CONTENTS

INTRODUCTION

What does it mean to be an awesome employee? In a nutshell, awesome employees know themselves, manage themselves, and build strong relationships with the folks around them. They are great team players who encourage others and take initiative to make things better. All of these elements fit together. Poor self-awareness = poor self-management, and self-management is a must for relationship building. The 25 exercises in this book offer you some food for thought and practical challenges, as well as guidance for reflecting and learning from those experiences. If you want to become an awesome and amazingly fabulous employee, this book for you. If you're already pretty awesome, that's cool. At the very least, this book will give you a tune-up and help you tweak your awesomeness.

Why become an awesome employee? There's a lot of competition for relatively few jobs, so employers are becoming choosier about who they hire. Technical skills aren't enough. Employers are looking for people who have a positive attitude, who can manage themselves, and who work well with others. Self-starters. Positive vibes. People Skills. According to the employers interviewed by journalist Caroline Rodgers, employers are looking for employees who:

- Learn and evolve as individuals (openness)
- Show initiative (proactivity)
- Take responsibility (self-motivation, maturity)
- Are versatile and able to work in more than one area (resourcefulness)
- Work as a team, listen and accept the ideas of others (relationship oriented)
- Demonstrate integrity and follow rules (moral compass)
- Manage their emotions and thoughts (self-control)
- Show leadership (setting a good example)
- Adapt to change (adaptability).

Do all of these describe you? If not, don't worry. If you put effort into the exercises in this book, you'll develop some skills and insights that will help you become an awesome employee.

What's in it for you?	What's in it for your employer?
You'll enjoy your work more. Others will want to work with you. You'll be more motivated and productive (which always feels good). You'll feel less stress. You'll feel more "in control" of yourself. You'll have better performance reviews. Your supervisor and coworkers will like you. You'll be more likely to get promoted.	You'll be more motivated and productive. (which is why you're there). You'll be more creative and helpful. You'll be more respectful toward your supervisor and everyone else. You'll be able to work more independently. You'll "be part of the solution, not the problem." You'll help to build a strong team and a positive work environment.

WHAT'S IN THE BOOK

Part 1 will help you build your self-awareness. If you were asked, "Who are you?" how would you answer? You may think that self-awareness isn't a big deal, but, in fact, it's the prerequisite for a lot of other skills, such as self-management. Indeed, awesome employees have a good sense of who they are and who they are not. First of all, they have a personal idea of what it means to be an awesome employee. They know how their early experiences, whether as a child or on their first jobs, influence their expectations and behaviors in the workplace. Self-aware people place themselves in situations where they are working from their strengths. At the same time, they work on their weaknesses so that they can develop

3

as individuals. They accept that people are unique, and that differences, rather than being wrong, need to be appreciated and accommodated. They value themselves as individuals but not at the expense of those around them. They know what motivates them and what they want out of life, and they establish goals and plans to get there. They make things happen for themselves.

In Part 2, you'll develop some insight and skills to manage yourself. If you rated how well you manage yourself right now on a scale of 1 to 10, what would be your score? Do you think you're good at disciplining yourself, managing your time and stress levels, and managing your moods and attitudes? Keep in mind that everyone is a work in progress, so if you don't score a perfect 10, don't kick yourself. For their part, awesome employees don't need or expect others to pamper, coddle, prod, or motivate them. They're self-starters who take responsibility for themselves – what they feel, think, and do – rather than blaming others. They have positive attitudes and are pleasant to be around. They're able to evaluate how well their own behaviors are working for them and make plans for improvements.

Part 3 offers you exercises in building relationships. It focuses on how well you connect with others in your interactions. Awesome employees invest in great relationships with other people. They show interest in others, listen well, and don't throw out zingers that belittle others. They energize those around them rather than sapping them of energy. They take initiative to resolve conflicts or misunderstandings as soon as they appear.

In Part 4, you'll develop your skills as a team player and leader. Awesome employees are great team members. They know what they're looking for in a team and organizational setting. They collaborate with others, and they contribute well to team meetings and participate in decision making. They influence others in a positive manner. Awesome employees try to develop themselves so that their supervisors can delegate work to them instead of having to watch them closely. They adapt to changing work situations, and they are able to see when change is needed. They are aware of what causes them stress, and they know how to handle stress (before it handles them).

The two exercises in Part 5 help you integrate what you've learned throughout the journey of completing the exercises in this book.

HOW TO GET THE MOST OUT OF THE BOOK

"I hear and I forget. I see and I remember. I do and I understand." – Confucius

"Life is a succession of lessons which must be lived to be understood." – Emerson

What are the exercises about? Each exercise presents a challenge which asks you to take certain actions, sometimes by yourself and sometimes with the help of others. You're then invited to **reflect on what happened** during the exercise: What happened? What did you do? What were your reactions? Those of others? Next, you're asked to step back and **identify the lessons you learned**, given your experience in the exercise. Common questions at this point are: "So what?" and "Why is it important?" The final step is to **develop an action plan** so that you can build on these lessons in the future. This involves asking yourself what you'll do differently in the future. What will you continue to do? Do more of? Less of? The *final* final step, of course, is following through on your action plan, then evaluating how things went and figuring out what you need to do differently, if anything.

In order to truly learn from our experiences, we need to do a complete loop of the learning cycle: we need to reflect on our experiences, figure out what lessons we learned, consider ways to apply these lessons, and then apply the lessons. You may know people who repeat the same mistakes over and over again and never seem to learn from them. It's probably because they go through life without taking the time to reflect, consider what they've learned, and develop an action plan in order to change their experiences. They're stuck somewhere on the learning cycle. David Kolb, the creator of this experiential learning cycle, says that we all have a favorite part of the cycle where we tend to get stuck. Some of us think and think and continue to think without taking action. At the other extreme, some of us take action without first reflecting on our experiences and what we learned from them. In the same way, if you just read the description of the exercises and do nothing else, you won't experience them, and the learning process will get stuck off the bat.

So don't just read the book. Reading it won't transform you into an awesome employee. Just like learning to ride a bike, it's impossible to develop your skills by simply reading or even thinking about what you have read. You might get to know a lot about what it means to be an awesome employee without changing what you do in the workplace. How useful is that? Besides, as *The Matrix* reminds us, "There's a difference between knowing the path and walking it." You've got to DO the exercises to get any benefit from them, plain and simple.

How can you get the most out of this book? You can do one or two exercises per week for a few months. Ultimately, this will help you develop a better understanding of yourself as an employee, your expectations, strengths, and areas for improvement. As a way of refreshing your skills, you can even repeat the series of exercises in the future. On the other hand, since one exercise isn't a prerequisite for another, you could choose only those exercises that grab your attention. The risk of this approach is that you may miss out on exercises that could be great learning opportunities for you. Sometimes the exercises that appear to be least interesting to us are those that offer the best learning experiences. Finally, you could randomly select a few exercises from each part of the book. Write their numbers on pieces of paper, put them in a bowl, and pick one to start the next day.

Here are **three other important things** to do to maximize your learning. First, **keep a learning journal**. Record your thoughts as you carry out the challenges, answer the reflection questions, and develop your action plans.  It will help you clarify your thinking, see patterns in what you have been experiencing and writing, and serve as a record of commitments you've made to yourself through your action plans. You will be able to look back at what you've written and be impressed with all that you've learned! If your learning journal is electronic, you'll be able to create a cool word cloud that reveals themes in your experiences (see exercise 25).

Second, **pull together a feedback team** that will help you get the most from the exercises. It could include your coworkers, your supervisor, friends, family, anyone that you have confidence in. Don't be shy about asking people for their support in helping you  become an awesome employee; they are more willing to help you than you might think! Besides, several exercises in this book ask you to get feedback from others or to share your reflections with them. These discussions will offer you different perspectives on the exercises and exponentially increase how much you learn from them. It will be interesting to see how each person can interpret an exercise differently from one another. Besides, awesome employees surround themselves with people they trust who are willing to give them honest feedback that will help them grow as individuals.

Third, **develop and implement a SMART action plan.**

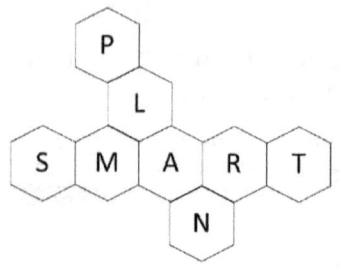

You know you've really learned something when your behavior has changed (for the better, of course). Exercises that are meaningful to you will change not only your perspectives, but also your behaviors. That's why each exercise ends by inviting you to develop an action plan. Your plan should be **S**pecific, **M**easurable, **A**ttainable, **R**ealistic, and **T**imely. Think about things that you need to start doing, stop doing, or continue doing. Here's an example: "By the end of next week, I will write two letters – one to my former supervisor and one to my best friend – expressing my gratitude for their coaching and willingness to challenge me to become a better person. I will send these letters by email no later than Saturday afternoon." Write your action plan in your journal, and revisit it to check your progress and revise your plan as needed. Remember to ask for help from others, to evaluate your progress within a specific period of time, and to reward yourself for your progress toward becoming an awesome employee.

How can you motivate yourself? First of all, keep in mind that to really learn from the exercises, you need to make a serious effort to carry them out. No one's going to hand you learning on a silver platter. Don't wait to be motivated to start an exercise. Start an exercise, and motivation will come knocking at your door! Tell yourself that you'll invest 10 minutes, and at the end of 10 minutes, if you're not even somewhat interested in the exercise, give yourself permission to move on. Also, try to be comfortable with discomfort. It's natural if an exercise makes you a bit uncomfortable in one way or another. It may be tempting to give up when things feel unnatural, but rest assured that this is part of the learning process. Sometimes, we come across awesome folks who do their work without hesitation and seemingly without effort. It's easy to forget that they've gone through the highs and lows of the learning process. For example, think of Cirque du Soleil acrobats who seem to perform stunts with ease and pinpoint accuracy. It took them lots of practice, repetition, and even occasional failures to get to that skill level. Experts make things look easy.

Are you ready to begin your awesome journey? Earl Nightingale once said, "All you need is the plan, the road map, and the courage to press on to your destination." I hope that this book serves as your guide and road map on your journey toward awesomeness.

~If you want to have an awesome day,
do something awesome every day. ~

PART 1:
KNOWING
YOURSELF

1

ARE YOU AN AWESOME EMPLOYEE?

"We are what we repeatedly do. Excellence then, is not an act, but a habit." – Aristotle

"Do all the good you can, by all the means you can, in all the ways you can, in all the places you can, at all the times you can, to all the people you can, as long as ever you can." – John Wesley

How would you define what it means to be an awesome employee? How would your supervisor (if you have one) define it? Everyone has their own perspectives about what works and what doesn't work in the workplace based on their past experiences. But, as you'll see in this exercise, a few essentials are common to all awesome employees. Are you afraid that you might not be an awesome employee? That the habits that you've picked up over time have caused you to stray from your essential awesomeness? If so, you're

like most people, so don't worry. We all have room to grow, and the starting point is figuring out where you stand on the awesomeness continuum.

Admittedly, developing an accurate self-perception and asking for honest feedback can be uncomfortable. Self-deception often blocks our having an accurate view of ourselves. We may think that we're completely awesome, but others might see us in a different light. We might fool ourselves to protect our self-image, and we may also be afraid to hear what others have to say. Sometimes, people don't give us feedback because we haven't asked for it, or they think that we might take it poorly. They're afraid to stick their neck out and ruin the relationship. So they give us "feedback lite." Instead of pointing out our less than stellar behaviors and tendencies that could derail our careers and lives (for example, complaining, avoiding work, or back talking), they might say something neutral (for example, "you bring a different perspective to situations"). Feedback lite won't point you in the direction of awesomeness. This exercise challenges you to step outside of your comfort zone and figure out where you stand.

Here's your two-part challenge: First, think about your behavior at work over the past two weeks. If you don't have a job, think about what you do while volunteering or at school. Now, check off any of the following behaviors of awesome employees that describe YOUR behavior during this time period. (Note: some of these behaviors are part of a work maturity list that Bettina Lankard and her colleagues prepared to help new employees adjust to the workplace.)

Awesome Employee Checklist

I'm punctual and present!

- I show up to work on time every day.
- I don't leave work early.
- I go to work every day.
- I call in sick only when I'm actually sick.
- I'm on time and prepared for meetings.
- I don't take extra-long lunch or coffee breaks.
- I concentrate on work while at work.

I have a positive attitude!

- I demonstrate interest and initiative in my work.
- I'm flexible, optimistic, and solution-oriented.
- I take responsibility for myself, and I demonstrate self-control.
- I don't moan or complain and bring everyone down with me.
- I don't spread rumors, gossip or mean jokes.
- I don't demean or "throw shade" on others.
- I admit my mistakes, and I try to learn from them.
- I manage my stressful feelings instead of spreading them around.
- I have a good sense of humor.
- I try to enjoy my work. If I don't like it, I change my attitude (I'm grateful for what is good about my job), I change what I do (I talk to my supervisor about it), or I move on.
- I say good things about my employer. I don't bad-mouth them on Facebook or elsewhere. If I don't want to work there anymore, I give my notice and leave. But, while I'm there, I try to make things better.

I develop positive interpersonal relations!

- I communicate honestly and diplomatically.
- I show interest in others.
- I accept constructive criticism.
- I interact appropriately with and am respectful toward others.
- I avoid aggression, inappropriate comments, and backbiting.
- I cooperate with and support my supervisor; I don't talk back to my supervisor.
- I work well with people from diverse backgrounds.
- I try to include everyone in conversations; I make sure that no one's left out.
- I solve any conflicts or misunderstandings through constructive problem solving.
- I help to build team spirit and contribute to the group effort.
- My emails are succinct, polite and positive.

I get my work done!

- I follow verbal and written instructions/directions.
- I do the right job. If I'm unclear about what to do, I ask for help right away (instead of hoping that I'll figure it out or doing a sloppy job).
- I begin work promptly and stay on task.
- I complete assigned tasks at an acceptable pace and on time.
- I do my work fast enough that I don't keep people waiting.
- I try to find efficient ways to do my work.
- I do the job right. I do my work carefully, correctly, and thoroughly.
- I'm organized, I plan my work, and I meet deadlines without a last-minute rush.
- I work independently without needing constant supervision, direction, and encouragement.

14

- I motivate myself to get my work done.
- I don't slack off when my supervisor isn't around.
- I recognize problems and develop solutions.
- I don't pass off work to others.
- I don't pretend to be busy.
- I don't waste other people's time.
- I don't take credit for other people's accomplishments.
- I keep my supervisor informed.

I'm responsible when using my employer's stuff.
- I don't steal money, stuff, or time.
- Office supplies stay at the office.
- I don't do personal emailing, photocopying, or printing at work.
- I don't pad my expense statements.
- I put away my cell phone, and I don't consult Facebook, YouTube, or other websites unless it's for work.
- I wait until my break or after work to do any personal business.
- I treat equipment and property with care.
- I work safely.
- I use materials wisely to avoid waste.
- I keep a neat work area.
- I clean up after myself in the lunch room and elsewhere.
- I don't fool around and do monkey business at work (unless I'm a zookeeper, of course).

I try to look professional.
- I maintain a reasonable level of personal hygiene (grooming).
- I wear appropriate clothing (dress).
- I keep my appearance neat (clothes, hair, shoes, nails, etc.).
- I don't groom myself while at work; I arrive at work fully groomed and ready to work.

15

Now that you've taken a few minutes to assess yourself, your **second step** is to ask at least two people (your coworkers or your supervisor) to check the items on the Awesome Employee Checklist that describe you. The more feedback the better! If you get lots of people to complete the checklist for you, you'll be able to look for trends in their responses. Let them know that this is part of your personal development process and that you appreciate their help. It might be hard to ask for their feedback, but you will appreciate it once you have it. At the very least, it will let you know how they see you. If there are any misperceptions, this will be your chance to clear them up. Or they might ask you for feedback. Whatever happens, a line of communication will be opened. Keep track of your results in your journal.

Reflection: Answer the following questions in your journal: How did you feel during this exercise? How many items did you check on the Awesome Employee Checklist? In reviewing the unchecked items, what reasons do you have for not doing them? For example, do you work with others who are a bad influence on you? Does no one seem to care what you do? Are you bored and looking for distractions? Are you lazy? Something else? Try to figure out what's stopping you from doing these awesome things. How difficult was it to ask for help from others? What was their response? Now, look at the checklists that others have completed and compare them with yours. What are the differences and similarities? How might you explain any differences in opinion? Ask your feedback team to help you analyze these differences and similarities. What do the overall results say about you as an employee? What are your strengths and weaknesses? What do you need to do more or less of, and what do you need to continue doing to become an awesome employee? What lessons have you learned in doing this exercise?

Action plan: Given your reflections, choose three behaviors that you're willing to start doing and stop doing today that will help you become more awesome. It's a good idea to plan to re-do the Awesome Employee Checklist in the near future and have others complete it as well as a way of evaluating your progress. Keep a record of your plan and your progress in your journal.

2

WHEN YOU WERE GROWING UP, WHAT DID YOU LEARN ABOUT BEING A GOOD EMPLOYEE?

"My earliest memories of my father are of seeing him work at his desk and realizing that he was happy. I did not know it then, but that was one of the most precious gifts a father can give his child." – Malcolm Gladwell

"Every experience in your life is being orchestrated to teach you something you need to know to move forward." – Brian Tracy

When Sue reflects on her earliest memories about the world of work, her father's daily accounts of his work day at the dinner table come to mind. Her father, Robert, was a factory foreman, "one of the guys," someone who enjoyed working hard and going for a beer with the guys after work. Sue felt nostalgic: she could see her parents sitting at the ends of the table, her brothers across from her, and her sister next to her. On the table was the standard fare of boiled potatoes, canned beets, very well cooked pork chops, and thoroughly boiled carrots, as well as slices of homemade bread with large crusts (that she would hide under her sister's plate). Her father would wash his hands, and dinner would be served at exactly 5 p.m. every day.

He would tell Sue, her siblings, and her mother about the happenings at the workplace – the big orders from a faraway country, the expansion of the factory, and the exciting times when the business owner would tour the shop and show appreciation for the work done by Robert and his colleagues. Yes, they were more like colleagues because Robert hated the idea of hierarchy, one person bossing another around. He made sure that everyone knew what to do, and he worked alongside them making parts,

19

occasionally taking the time to help someone operate a lathe or something else. He was there to help. He ate lunch with the guys and shared rides with them to the shop. Sue would hear happy stories of celebrations of major shipments, sad stories of employees being injured, and exhausting stories about working overtime to fulfill orders.

Working alongside the guys, working hard, getting along, and being loyal and humble were Robert's trademarks. One year, Robert won the employee of the year award; he was handed a very expensive bright red leather jacket with a huge arm patch that said "EMPLOYEE OF THE YEAR." Robert graciously accepted the jacket, but he was embarrassed to wear it and never did. He attributed the success of the factory to the guys, and wearing the jacket would make it look like he thought he was special. A dedicated employee, Robert worked until one fateful day when he injured his back and could no longer work. Leaving his job was overdue; the new owner of the business was putting pressure on employees to work much, much harder than ever and to undergo complex training about complex work processes. Also, he didn't tour the shop to show that he cared about the employees and their work.

When Sue thought about how she learned about working and being an awesome employee, her father's example came to mind. Here's what she learned:

- Good employees work hard and are dedicated to their employers.
- Good leaders are egalitarian: they treat their employees as colleagues rather than as subordinates.
- They leave employees alone to do their work but help when needed. They're available and helpful; not overbearing.
- They offer appropriate recognition to employees: informal and ongoing expressions of appreciation are better than one-time awards that may single out and embarrass people.

- Celebrating successes and being supportive during hard times were important elements of life at work.
- Getting to know your employees as people with families and lives outside the workplace and letting them get to know you in the same way builds a solid bridge of understanding.
- Building solid relationships with others not only helps you get the work done but it also makes the workplace more humane.
- Being able to read the "writing on the wall" and taking action so that you can take care of yourself is important. Don't assume that others have your best interests at heart. Unfortunately some people will take advantage, and you need to know when to stay, when to fight, and when to go.

Sue was proud of her father and knew that he was proud of his work. He was always so excited to give a little tour of the shop to his kids every once in a while. But Sue was also sad that the last few years of her father's time at the factory had been especially challenging. She vowed to pay special attention to the organizational memory and special dedication offered by long-term employees. These memories remain etched in Sue's heart. When faced with workplace dilemmas, she often asks herself what her father would do, because she knows that he always did the right thing, with one exception (not looking out for himself).

What are your reactions to Sue's story? How do you think her experience shaped her perception of what it means to be an awesome employee? A great way to figure out what being an awesome employee means to you is to mine your past; in other words, to reflect on your personal or work experiences as an employee, as a volunteer or athlete, or even around the dinner table with your family as Sue did. Our first exposures to the world of work tend to mark us, create expectations for what the world of work should be like, and become the basis for comparing the rest of our experiences. This is especially true of significant experiences in our lives; we carry them around with us, usually without even being aware of doing so.

According to Dr. William Glasser's choice theory, it helps to imagine that we are carrying around a photo album in our heads; an album that contains pictures of all our best and preferred experiences. As we go about our day-to-day lives, we're constantly and unconsciously comparing what's in our photo albums with what we're experiencing. When there's a match, it feels good. No action is needed; we soak in this feeling that everything is right in the world. When there's a mismatch, we can sense it; we know that something's not quite right, and we figure out what to do. We might try to influence the experience, just accept it, or avoid it.

Here's your challenge: Think about your early role models of awesome employees. These could be your parents, grandparents, your first supervisor, or anyone else whose path you crossed on a day-to-day basis. Just as Sue did above, prepare an anecdote about your earliest exposure to the world of working. Share this story with your feedback team, and ask for their help in interpreting it and distilling its key lessons. Write your story and comments from your feedback team in your journal.

Reflection: Answer the following questions in your journal. How did you feel when you prepared your anecdote? How did reflecting on your early experiences help you to understand them and put them in perspective? What did your early experiences teach you about what it means to be an awesome employee? How has your personal anecdote influenced your expectations of your jobs and your supervisors and what you think it means to be an awesome employee? What recurring themes do you see in your personal story?

Action plan: Based on your personal anecdote, describe the five most important actions that you will take and the five most important actions that you will avoid to get you closer to being an awesome employee starting now. These actions can serve as key principles that guide your attitudes and behaviors at work and elsewhere. Keep a record of your plan and your progress in implementing your plan in your journal.

3

DO YOU HAVE THE PERSONALITY OF AN AWESOME EMPLOYEE?

"Be yourself. Everyone else is already taken." – Oscar Wilde

"Always be yourself, express yourself, have faith in yourself, do not go out and look for a successful personality and duplicate it."
– Bruce Lee

What kind of personalities do awesome employees have, you might ask. Don't worry; there isn't one ideal personality, but there are ranges of personality traits that are more effective than others. The most common way of thinking about personality is using the Big 5 personality traits. Using the acronym OCEAN, the traits are **O**penness to experience, **C**onscientiousness, **E**xtraversion, **A**greeableness, and **N**euroticism. This exercise will help you figure out your personality profile including your strengths and some areas for development.

Here's your challenge: Before delving into this topic any further, reflect on your own personality. Look at the table on the next page and shade or color in those cells that accurately reflect who you are (not who you want to be). Think about how you generally are; not what you think you should be or those times when you are super relaxed or under significant stress. Now ask three people who know you very well (possibly your feedback team) to do the same. Don't reveal your personal assessment to your feedback team; this might influence their assessments.

There are four copies of the personality table on the following pages: one for you and three for your feedback team. Tear out the three pages containing the Personality Table Exercise (copies 1, 2, and 3) and give them to your feedback team. Once your feedback team has completed their tables, continue on to the rest of the instructions for this exercise.

Personality Table Exercise
(your copy)

Instructions: For each dimension, place an X in the cell that best fits with how you generally are (not when you are relaxed or stressed). Explain your choices in the Comments section.

	7	6	5	4	3	2	1
	Extremely high	Very high	High	Middle-of-the-road	Somewhat low	Low	Extremely low
Openness to experience creative, curious, open-minded							
Conscientiousness self-directed, responsible, reliable, persevering							
Extraversion talkative, active, sociable, outgoing							
Agreeableness kind, trusting cooperative, appreciative							
Neuroticism irritable, defensive, sensitive, fearful							

Personality Table Exercise
(copy #1)

Instructions: Think about the person who asked you to fill in this table. For each dimension, place an X in the cell that best fits with how they generally are (not when they are relaxed or stressed). Explain your choices in the Comments section.

	7	6	5	4	3	2	1
	Extremely high	Very high	High	Middle-of-the-road	Somewhat low	Low	Extremely low
Openness to experience creative, curious, open-minded							
Conscientiousness self-directed, responsible, reliable, persevering							
Extraversion talkative, active, sociable, outgoing							
Agreeableness kind, trusting cooperative, appreciative							
Neuroticism irritable, defensive, sensitive, fearful							

Comments (examples/rationale for my ratings):

Personality Table Exercise
(copy #2)

Instructions: Think about the person who asked you to fill in this table. For each dimension, place an X in the cell that best fits with how they generally are (not when they are relaxed or stressed). Explain your choices in the Comments section.

	7	6	5	4	3	2	1
	Extremely high	Very high	High	Middle-of-the-road	Somewhat low	Low	Extremely low
Openness to experience creative, curious, open-minded							
Conscientiousness self-directed, responsible, reliable, persevering							
Extraversion talkative, active, sociable, outgoing							
Agreeableness kind, trusting cooperative, appreciative							
Neuroticism irritable, defensive, sensitive, fearful							

Comments (examples/rationale for my ratings):

Personality Table Exercise
(copy #3)

Instructions: Think about the person who asked you to fill in this table. For each dimension, place an X in the cell that best fits with how they generally are (not when they are relaxed or stressed). Explain your choices in the Comments section.

	7	6	5	4	3	2	1
	Extremely high	Very high	High	Middle-of-the-road	Somewhat low	Low	Extremely low
Openness to experience creative, curious, open-minded							
Conscientiousness self-directed, responsible, reliable, persevering							
Extraversion talkative, active, sociable, outgoing							
Agreeableness kind, trusting cooperative, appreciative							
Neuroticism irritable, defensive, sensitive, fearful							

31

Comments (examples/rationale for my ratings):

Did the members of your feedback team complete the personality tables? If not, follow up with them; it's worth the effort. When the tables are completed, you'll need to merge all the results onto your own table. Then, you need to determine your average rating for each personality trait. Keep track of the assessments, your merged table, and your average scores in your journal.

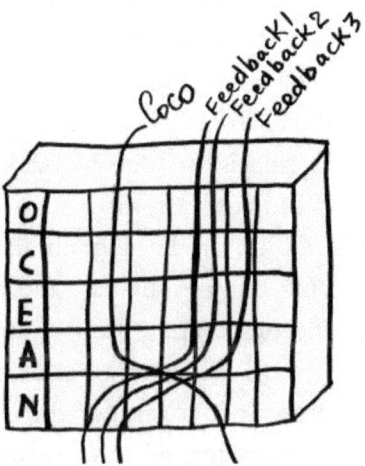

For example, Coco gave herself a score of 6 in extraversion and her feedback team gave her 3, 3, and 2. Coco's average rating for extraversion is 3.5 (6 + 3 + 3 + 2 divided by 4 people), which is 2.5 points lower than Coco's own assessment. Coco calculated her average score for each personality trait and obtained the following results: 3.5 in openness to experience, 3.5 in conscientiousness, 3.5 in agreeability, and 5.25 in neuroticism. In the diagram, we can see that Coco's personal evaluation differs significantly from that of her feedback team. Coco should think about why her personal perceptions are so different from those of others. Does she tend to overestimate the positive aspects of her personality? Does she have poor self-awareness and is really unsure of her personality?

Now, here's more information about each of the personality traits according to personality researchers Oliver John and Sanjay Srivastava.

People who are moderately high in **Openness to Experience** tend be very curious about the world around them. They are imaginative, innovative, inventive, original, and creative. They're open-minded, open to change, flexible, open to others' perspectives, and open to new ideas and possibilities. They have a wide range of interests, possibly including art, literature, and music. Typically, openness to experience has been associated with increased creativity in the workplace. However, when excessive, openness to experience is a recipe for disaster. Too much openness leads to unpredictability, reckless risk taking, too much flexibility (inconsistency), and indecision (due to being open to too many options/possibilities). In contrast, those who are somewhat low on this scale tend to be a bit more hesitant about newness and out-of-the-box ways of doing things. They are more traditional and will spend some time reflecting on new ideas or approaches, but will be open to moving forward when rational explanations have been offered. At the "extremely low" end of the continuum lies **close-mindedness**. It's characterized by rigidity, inflexibility, an unwillingness to change, a narrow range of interests, and not listening to others' ideas. Awesome employees tend to be moderately high in openness to experiences.

Conscientiousness is the *piece de resistance* of personality; it's the key trait that determines success in life (including personal health) and in the workplace. Along with extraversion and openness to experience, it's associated with leadership emergence (the possibility of becoming a leader). People who are moderately high in conscientiousness are self-disciplined, organized, perseverant, thorough, methodical, analytical, responsible, reliable, dependable, achievement-oriented hard workers. They're able to control their impulses, think before they act, delay gratification, and follow rules and norms. If overdone (extremely high), **"maladaptive" conscientiousness** can lead to obsessing about details, excessive cautiousness, stubbornness, nit-picking, rigidity, compulsions, and obsessions (for example, extreme orderliness). Its opposite, **impulsiveness,** is characterised by neglect, carelessness, disorganization, frivolousness, irresponsibleness, undependability, unreliability, forgetfulness about one's commitments, distractibility, laziness, rule breaking, risk taking, and impulsive behaviors (in relation to spending, driving, sex, eating, and other habits). Such individuals are easily bored and tend to act on the spur of the moment without thinking through their actions. Awesome employees are likely to have a very high/high conscientiousness score.

Those who are moderately high in **Extraversion** tend to be talkative, sociable, active, outspoken, energetic, enthusiastic, excitement seeking, and outgoing. They like to be the center of attention. In contrast, those who are somewhat low on this scale, **introverts**, dislike drawing attention to themselves. They tend to be low-key folks (especially around people they don't know), quiet, reserved, calm, reflective, and thoughtful. They like to think before they speak, and they tend to be good listeners. Independent minded, they also prefer small groups and need time alone to re-energize themselves. As you can imagine, all of the qualities just mentioned describe awesome employees. You can be an extravert or an introvert and be an awesome employee. Although some introverts feel inadequate in this extraverted world, they need to realize that they can be awesome employees who quietly make the world a better place. They simply have their own way of being involved in the social world around them (just as extraverts do). The middle range of the extraversion scale (somewhat high to somewhat low) is where you'll find awesome employees. Over-the-top extraverts tend to have trouble listening because they are so busy talking. They may also live most of their lives in the outer world of people and action and, as a result, have trouble reflecting before acting and developing an awareness of themselves (intrapersonal skills). They can have difficulty being alone and may even be intrusive toward

35

others when seeking social interaction. At their very worst, they can become narcissistic, bossy show-offs who dominate conversations and others. Extreme introverts, on the other hand, tend to shut themselves in from social interactions. They may be withdrawn and avoidant, distant and disengaged, inhibited, shy, and downright reclusive. It's best to avoid the extremes of this scale.

Individuals who are high in **Agreeableness** are sympathetic, considerate, warm, appreciative, good natured, trusting, forgiving, likeable, modest (not boastful), kind, gentle, cooperative, helpful, soft-hearted, affectionate, generous, and unselfish. They are the all-around "good guy" that people like to be around and to have as a friend, coworker, or even supervisor. Is it possible to be too agreeable? It depends. If agreeable people are excessively compliant and trusting, people may take advantage of them. Excessively agreeable folks can also have trouble making difficult decisions, especially those involving other people. Such folks need to learn to balance their agreeableness with a strong backbone: be kind AND able to make tough choices. On the opposite end of the continuum are people who lack agreeableness and are **antagonistic**. They may be unkind, mistrusting, fault-finding, thankless, unfriendly, hard-hearted, critical, and stubborn. At their worst, they are rude, contemptuous, hostile, quarrelsome, revenge-seeking, rigid, manipulative, cold, calculating, callous, and cunning. At their very worst, they are antisocial and paranoid of everyone around them. Awesome employees are likely to have a very high/high agreeableness score.

Finally, **Neuroticism** at moderate to high levels is characterized by pessimism, anxiety, tenseness, nervousness, depression, defensiveness, irritability, vulnerability, excessive worrying, fearfulness, insecurity, high-strung reactivity, self-pitying, moodiness, emotionality, and quick loss of temper. Such individuals are easily upset, temperamental, and prone to distress. They experience and express excessive negative emotions and have strong adverse emotional reactions to day-to-day stresses. Distress, reduced psychological and physical health, poor job performance, and relationship problems are characteristic of people with high levels of neuroticism. They are sensitive and likely to (unduly) take things personally. In contrast, individuals with high levels of **emotional stability**, the opposite end of the neuroticism scale, are even-tempered, calm, contented, not easily upset, relaxed, and optimistic. They handle stress well by putting things in perspective. Awesome employees are likely to have a low/extremely low neuroticism score. Together, high levels of agreeableness and emotional stability are associated with high performance in jobs requiring group work. The opposite is also true: if you have high levels of neuroticism and low agreeableness, not only will you have poor personal health, but your performance in a group setting will suffer as well.

  Now to interpret your results. The first thing to remember is that there is a **range of levels** for each of the personality traits. It's not a question of "you've either got it or you don't." For example, you can be a blend of extraversion and introversion, depending on your comfort and energy levels in a social situation. Second, any of the personality traits that are **significantly overdone** (extremely high) or **significantly underdone** (extremely low) tend to be unhealthy. This means that even *positive* traits in the extremes can be detrimental (except for emotional stability, of course). Third, sometimes when we experience **extreme stress**, our behavior is likely to be out of character. People might say that they are not "being themselves." This is why it's important to consider your behavior on average. Having said this, it can be useful to consider your "Stress Personality Profile;" in other words, what you're like when you're stressed. For example, do you generally score a 1 in neuroticism but, under extreme stress, it jumps to 7? Fourth, although personality is considered to be relatively stable, it's possible to develop aspects of your personality by changing your patterns of thinking and behaving so that you have **more positive outcomes**. It's not set in stone. Fifth, it can be helpful to look at your combination of results on the Big 5 traits. As a group, what do they say about you? Researchers Oliver John and Sanjay Srivastava found links between three combinations and psychological adjustment. *Resilients* had moderately high levels of openness, conscientiousness, extraversion, and agreeableness, and high levels of emotional stability. They had the best results for psychological adjustment (in other words, positive mental health). In contrast, both *Overcontrollers* and *Undercontrollers* had poor psychological adjustment. Anxious *Overcontrollers* include those with high levels of Agreeableness and Conscientiousness but low levels of Extraversion. Conflicted *Undercontrollers* are those with low levels of Agreeableness and Conscientiousness and high levels of Neuroticism.

Why should you care about personality? Well, it affects what you think, say, and do, all of which influence the impact that you have as an employee. Understanding your personality will help you understand yourself better, which helps you accept yourself and appreciate your strengths and weaknesses. People feel more energy and positive emotions and perform better when they are using their strengths. So, understanding your personality will help you choose a career where you can prosper rather than simply survive. As well, if you're aware of your weaknesses, you can become more aware of situations that call on your weaknesses and that drain your energy. You can work on your weaknesses so that they don't get in your way of becoming an awesome employee.

We are all a combination of strengths and weaknesses. According to Rob Goffee and Gareth Jones, trying to look perfect comes across as conceited and fake. Showing that you're not perfect and that you have particular quirks (such as needing concentrated desk time) can actually make you more likeable to others. At the same time, fully disclosing of all your weaknesses is likely to undermine how others see you. Your team mates don't need to know that you're afraid of heights (unless you're a sky diver, of course) or that you have a problem with excessive gas.

Reflection: Answer the following questions in your journal. Looking at your results, how would you describe your personality? What strengths and weaknesses do you have? What special strengths do you have that are central to what you have to offer your employer? In other words, what sets you apart from the pack? What weaknesses are you comfortable disclosing to others? How might your strengths and weaknesses influence your ability to be an awesome employee? How does your personal assessment fit with how others have assessed you? Were there any surprises? Sometimes we don't show the real "us" to others, so they get a distorted picture of who we are. At the same time, sometimes others are able to recognize our strengths and weaknesses better than we can ourselves. If you're confused about the feedback that you've received from others, ask them for examples so that you know why they consider you an extreme extravert, for example.

Action plan:
1. **Build on your strengths:** Do you ever look at someone who seems to have it all? This person seems to be popular, have a way with other people, and attract success at every turn. It might be tempting to try to be like that person, but, as the earlier quote from Oscar Wilde suggests, being the best version of yourself that you can be is the best thing to do. Award-winning photographer Chase Jarvis suggests that we need to find and build on our mojo, which is our unique combination of strengths. It's something that no one else has. We need to ask ourselves, "What is the mojo that I bring, and how can I build on it?" How would you respond to that question based on your personality strengths?

2. **Deal with your weaknesses:** Everyone has weaknesses or areas that need to be developed. In considering your weaknesses, what five precise actions will you take starting now to address them? For example, will you become more open to experiences, conscientious, and agreeable (but not overly so), be able to balance expressiveness and introspection, and increase your level of emotional stability? These are all areas that can be developed with conscious effort. If you have low levels of openness, what steps will you take to embrace different perspectives more frequently? If you're an introvert, you might consider doing an experiment in which you "act bold, talkative, energetic, active, assertive, and adventurous." According to John Zelenski, Maya Santoro, and Deanna Whelan of Carleton University, introverts feel better after acting like they're extraverted. It's a classic "fake it till you make it" scenario. On the other hand, if you're an extravert, what are you going to do to become more reflective and calm? It's been said that, because we live in an extraverted society, introverts are used to having to express themselves in social situation. However, extraverts can find it especially challenging to be reflective. Both are needed to achieve balance in life. Yin and yang.

3. **Build your level of self-awareness:** It's important to continue to look for ways to build your self-awareness. Assessing your personality is one of many things that you can do to become more aware of who you are as a person. Rob Goffee and Gareth Jones suggest four major approaches: (a) actively pursuing new experiences and challenges; doing things outside your comfort zone; (b) seeking out frank feedback that will help you grow as a person; (c) reading biographies as a way of seeing how great leaders have dealt with their strengths and weaknesses; and (d) understanding the influence of your past, especially significant events, on your current behavior. What specific actions will you take starting now in this regard?

4. **Take feedback seriously:** When people take the time to give you feedback, it's important to take it seriously. Identify a recurring element of their feedback that you're interested in changing. This could be a positive perception (maybe they think you're nicer than you really are) or a negative perception (maybe they think you're moody). Consider the reasons for these perceptions, and what you may have done to contribute to their development. Identify three actions that you will take starting now that would inspire them to change any perceptions.

Keep a record of your plans and your progress in implementing them in your journal.

Here are some additional tips for developing your personality:

- Take time to reflect before making decisions. Don't act like a chicken with your head cut off by taking action or making decisions without first thinking them through. Don't rush into decisions, but don't dawdle unnecessarily either. Avoid analysis paralysis: sometimes you've got to move on!
- Keep things in perspective, step back and look at the big picture. Don't get lost in the trees without seeing the forest that you're in. At the same time, if you have an overall impression of a situation, ask yourself on what facts you're basing this impression.
- Learn from every situation. Reflect, find the lessons that a situation presents, plan to change your behavior, and then do it. That's how people grow in confidence and maturity.
- Don't impose your way of doing things on others. It's not your way or the highway. Try to see things from others' perspectives. Understand that everyone has their own way of seeing things. Just because they're different doesn't mean they're wrong.
- Appreciate your strengths. Find a job where you mainly use your strengths. Avoid jobs that ask you to use your weaknesses (for example, working in sales, if you're an introvert).

- Admit your weaknesses. Everyone's got them. Look at what you can do to deal with them so that they don't become "fatal flaws" that drag your career down and you with it.

- Get out and talk to people, even in small groups. Express your ideas. It's okay to plan what you say ahead of time. Realize that the only way to feel more comfortable around other people is to be around other people – a little at a time.

- Don't bulldoze your way through conversations; no one appreciates domineering people who don't seem to be sensitive to others' reactions to them. You may think that you're being "expressive," but others may not share your opinion. Be aware of the impact that you're having on others. If you talk too much, stop talking and take the time to listen to others. Try to reflect before speaking or acting. Show interest in others. Ask them questions.

- Live a little, and be open to new experiences. Unless you make an effort to open yourself up and try new things, your world will remain very small. If you're closed to new experiences, you won't grow as a person.

- Be reliable, responsible, and hardworking. Follow through on your commitments. If you have trouble doing this, here's a Yoda reality check: a successful career you shall not have.

- Be conscientious but not over the top. Don't go overboard with paying attention to details. Perfection does not exist in this world. Expecting perfection in yourself and others is a recipe for failure. Besides, people who are hard on others are usually really hard on themselves as well.

- Go along to get along. If you're a hostile, miserable fart who has trouble getting along with others, ease up on yourself and others. People are generally quite nice once you get to know them. Be friendly, pleasant, polite, and agreeable toward others, and they will generally do the same in return.

- If you're excessively nice, watch that others don't take advantage of your niceness. Not everyone plays fair, and you might get run over by manipulative people who won't hesitate to use you to their advantage. Be willing to stand up for yourself and set some boundaries. If people are asking you to do their work for them or if they consistently fail to do what they say they would do, you need to address the situation.

- If you're prone to being moody or feeling down or anxious, look into cognitive behavioral therapy. Cognitive behavioral therapy helps people who have trouble coping with their emotions. Don't want to do that? Then, at the very least, find a good book on this topic (there are lots available), and try to manage your emotions so that they are constructive and positive.

4
....

ARE YOU SELF-ABSORBED?

"There is no smaller package in all the world
than that of a man all wrapped up in himself."
– William Sloane Coffin

"People that know they are important, think about others. People
that think they are important, think about themselves."
– Hans F. Hansen

"You can make more friends in two months by becoming
interested in other people than you can in two years by trying to
get people interested in you." – Dale Carnegie

Well, no, of course you're not self-absorbed, but surely you know
someone who is: perhaps your coworker who sat next to you in the
lunch room and talked non-stop about herself for the entire time.
She talked about her experiences, her feelings, her opinions, her
possessions, her everything without inquiring about you. You
tried to be cordial, polite, gracious, possibly injecting a personal
opinion or story, but that didn't deter her from continuing. She
used any small display of interest on your part as an incentive to

44

launch into a lengthy monologue. As a result, you said little, out of fear of getting her started again. Was this dissatisfying conversation an isolated incident, or are you taken aback by the sheer number of people who seem to be interested primarily in "Me, Myself, and I"?

Self-absorption is clearly not well regarded. Self-absorbed folks are often avoided and resented. People may view them as being egotistical, narcissistic, or self-centered. Since they're less sensitive to others' needs, they are often the last to know the negative impressions that they leave with others. They may even think that they're wowing people with their exploits, but they are not. Self-absorbed people are all about themselves – what they want, what's convenient for them, their experience, their image, etc. What about the needs, wishes, and expectations of others? Meh! It goes without saying that awesome employees aren't self-absorbed. Nope! They're considerate folks who take an interest in the people and the world around them. And, they're aware of their impact on others.

You're probably self-absorbed, if you regularly:

- Hog talk time during conversations.
- Use the first person personal pronoun (I) excessively (for example, every second sentence).
- Focus on yourself without asking others questions.
- Relate everything others say back to you.
- Place yourself at the center of attention (if not, pout or check out of the conversation).
- Place your needs and comfort first (your preferences, the best seat, first in line, etc.).
- Interrupt others.
- Demand immediate attention from others.
- Look at yourself in the mirror a lot (like Coco)!

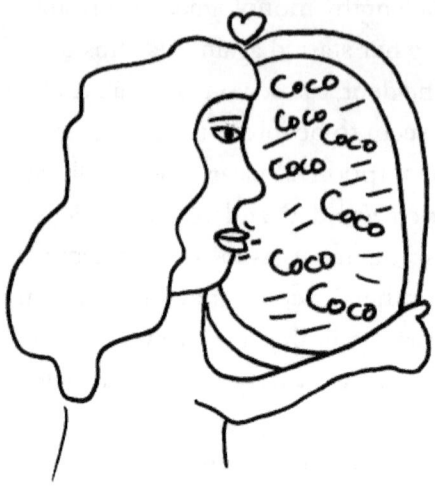

If you're feeling the pinch of recognition that you may be self-absorbed, what can you do? First of all, **realize that displaying a certain amount of self-valuing is natural and healthy.** It's a question of how much. Doing these things often tends to come across as a defense mechanism, a lack of self-acceptance, a cover-up for feelings of inadequacy (thus, the need to promote oneself), vulnerability, or an excessive need for external acceptance and affirmation. As communication expert Miles Sherts tells us, "There is an important distinction between self-absorption and self-care. When we are absorbed with ourselves, most of our energy goes into worrying about our needs and how to meet them. We tend to be on guard and more focused on what we lack than on what we have, which drains energy from ourselves and the people around us." Self-care is our capacity to care about ourselves and take responsibility for our own basic needs. Also, as John Yokoyama said in his popular book, *When Fish Fly*, "When we fear what other people think about us, we are frequently more focused on 'being interesting' and less focused on 'taking an interest.' That's why some people talk a lot when they're anxious and why many people never feel heard. If both people in the conversation are trying to be interesting, there is no one left to genuinely listen."

Second, beyond increasing your awareness of your self-absorption tendencies, you could try to **show more consideration of others** in future interpersonal interactions. For example:

- Monitor your talk time so that it's limited to a proportional share (for example, 50-50 in a two-person conversation).
- Show genuine interest in what others have to say (not only as it relates to you). Ask them questions and listen to what they're saying.
- Enjoy the flow of the conversation without directing it.
- Take care of others' needs and comfort (for example, arrive on time; offer others the best seat, the last slice of pizza, and the time they need to express themselves).
- Don't interrupt others when they're talking. Let them finish what they're asking.
- Don't force your opinion on others.
- Treat others like you would like to be treated.

Third, after having a conversation, feed it back in your mind and ask yourself how successful it was. Think about the kind of reactions that you received from others. Was it encouraging or rather brief as though they were trying to discourage further conversation? Did their eyes glaze over? Did they seem silent and passive or fully engaged? Did it look like they were trying to cut the conversation short or even escape? As a result of this reflection, you can identify specific ways to improve future conversations.

What are some options for dealing with self-absorbed folks? There are lots of books that you can consult to help you deal with self-absorption in general as well as in bosses, children, or even lovers. In the meantime, here are a few alternatives:

1. When this person is on a roll, try to **shift her attention by changing the topic of conversation**; for example: "That's really interesting Coco. By the way, have you noticed__"

2. **Call a time-out**; for example: "Wow, you must be really excited about your __. You've spent the last 20 minutes talking about it non-stop. I have some interesting news too."

3. **Clarify your needs in an assertive manner** in an attempt to ensure that both parties' needs are met, for example: "Coco, in our last conversation, you talked for about 30 minutes straight. I felt frustrated that I didn't have a chance to share with you what was happening in my life. In this conversation, how about if we make a conscious attempt to share talk time 50-50?"

4. **Clarify boundaries**. Set limits for what you will accept and what you will not accept, for example: "Coco, I only have about 5 minutes to chat with you because I have a commitment in 10 minutes." After 10 minutes, tell the person politely that you need to end the conversation, and do so.

5. In a non-confrontational, empathetic manner, **offer some feedback** on specific behaviors and their effects on you. Check the other person's awareness of their behaviors and their willingness to make specific changes. For example, "Hey Coco, would you be up for a bit of feedback?" If she says yes, "You may not be aware of this, but I noticed__."

These actions range in directness, potential effectiveness, and appropriateness depending on the kind of relationship you have with the self-absorbed person. Although it's not our role to change other people, we can teach them how we like to be treated. Whatever you decide, be gentle, remain positive, and show consideration.

Here's your three-part challenge: In part 1, we invite you to become aware of and modify your personal self-absorption tendencies. During three days this week, pay particular attention to any signs that suggest that you may be self-absorbed. Note your observations in your journal. **In part 2**, during the following four days, try to eliminate these behaviors from your behavioral repertoire, and engage in the behaviors presented in the second list (Monitor your talk time…). Take note of the effectiveness of your attempts as well as others' reactions. **In part 3**, to help you become more skilled in dealing with others' self-absorption tendencies, we invite you to practice the behaviors listed above (When this person is on a roll …) over a seven-day period. Note your attempts to do so as well as the reactions of others in your journal.

Reflection: Answer the following questions in your journal. How challenging was this exercise? What self-absorption tendencies were you able to identify in yourself? How effective were your attempts to eliminate these self-absorption habits and be more considerate of others? How did others react to the changes in your behaviors? Describe the incidents of self-absorption that you addressed, what you did, the effectiveness of your interventions, and others' reactions. What did you learn about yourself from this exercise?

Action plan: Now that you've had a chance to practice behaviors that show consideration of others and that challenge others' self-absorption habits, what do you commit to doing starting today to: (a) eliminate self-absorption behaviors from your repertoire; and (b) model considerate behavior? Keep a record of your plan and your progress in implementing your plan in your journal.

Food for thought:

- Think of others and their needs, rather than believing that the world should wait on you hand and foot. Realize that you may be the center of your universe, but you're not the center of someone else's universe.

- Try to see things from others' perspectives. Don't focus solely on your wants and desires or always place them first. You don't always have to get your way.
- Be generous with others, and others will be generous with you. You may not realize the impact that small gestures can have on others. Politeness, generosity, kindness, and gratitude are keys to building relationships with others.

5

DO YOU PLAY
THE BLAME GAME?

"An ignorant person is inclined to blame others for his own misfortune. To blame oneself is proof of progress. But the wise man never has to blame another or himself." – Epictetus

"The difference between great people and everyone else is that great people create their lives actively, while everyone else is created by their lives, passively waiting to see where life takes them next. The difference between the two is the difference between living fully and just existing." – Michael Gerber

"The commitments we make to ourselves and to others and our integrity to those commitments is the essence and clearest manifestation of our proactivity. It is also the essence of our growth. There are two ways to put ourselves in control of our lives immediately. We can make a promise – and keep it. Or, we can set a goal and work to achieve it. These give us the awareness of self-control and the courage and strength to accept more of the responsibility for our own lives." – Stephen Covey

Awesome employees don't engage in the blame game. They assume responsibility for themselves, for what happens to them, and for the decisions they make. In addition to being responsible for their own lives, they encourage the people around them to take responsibility without blaming, rescuing, or placating them. They establish relationships on an equal footing with others.

How about you? It's important to be aware of how you usually explain what happens to you. If you tend not to recognize your responsibility for your own life, you're likely to develop a feeling of helplessness or even fatalism. Are you the master of your life? Do you take responsibility for what's happening to you, including your successes and failures, or do you tend to blame others for anything that goes wrong? Where do you stand in the blame vs. responsibility game? Is it hard for you to accurately assess your responsibilities or blaming tendencies in a situation? Are you able to avoid the following attribution errors?

- **Overestimating your responsibility in a situation and underestimating the factors related to the situation and the context** (the fundamental attribution error). For example, if you're late for work, you blame yourself entirely.

- **Attributing your successes to personal factors (ability, intelligence, hard work) and your failures to unfavorable external factors (such as a lack of resources, bad weather, others' incompetence, etc.), but doing the opposite for others** (egocentric bias). For example, if you do well in a project, it's thanks to you. If the project isn't successful, you blame your supervisor. But, you attribute others' success to luck and their failures to personal incompetence.

These errors simplify the situation excessively and don't take into account all the factors that may be influencing the situation. Here are some examples of situations experienced by Coco and her friends Bob and Sue:

- Coco: I was late for work because the coffee shop line up was long, and the service was slow. I had planned 10 minutes to pick up coffee which finally took 20. Then I stopped to check my text messages on my cell phone, and I had to respond to a message from my sister about our plans for the weekend. So it wasn't my fault that I was late to work. On the other hand, Bob was late because he doesn't care about the time and he's super disorganized.

- Sue: My high level of performance in the first project was due to my hard work and my natural talent for teamwork. I wasn't as successful on the second project because my boss had unreasonable expectations, and there was just too much work to be done in a short period of time.

- Bob: I'm in my fifth job in three years. I changed jobs often because I had trouble working with incompetent and stupid people. I hope my new employer will be better, but I'm already disappointed because my boss seems to be a micro-manager who rarely shows appreciation for my amazing talents.

What's your interpretation of these situations? In the first example, Coco attributes her being late for work to solely external factors and Bob's lateness to internal factors. Do you think that Coco bears any responsibility for her lateness? For her part, Sue tends to think that her great performance is due to internal factors and her poor performance is due to external factors. As we saw in Exercise 2, she obviously didn't learn this from her father! As for Bob, he blames all the employment problems he has had over time to external factors for which he is not responsible. Do you agree? If the best predictor of future behavior is past behavior in similar circumstances, do you think that Bob will be quitting his current job in the near future (or staying but grumbling about the working conditions)?

How about you? Do you tend to blame others or circumstances, or do you take responsibility for *everything* that happens? **If you are continually in the "let's blame others" mode, then you probably have an external locus of control.** "Externals" think that the outside world is responsible for whatever happens to them: their failures, successes, and even neutral situations. According to externals, everything's out of their control, and they're victims of circumstance and other people. They're at the beck and call of others, chance, luck, flukes, misfortune – you name it! They don't make things happen; things happen to them. They put their rights before their responsibilities (not realizing that everyone has rights and responsibilities). They reject the idea that they may have some responsibility for their current situation.

In contrast, **people with an internal locus of control consider what happens to them to be their responsibility.** "Internals" don't blame others or circumstances or wait passively for good things to happen to them. These masters of destiny make things happen for themselves. They take action and responsibility for their part of what's happening, and they proactively work to improve their lot in life. Research clearly shows that developing an internal locus is the way to go. In contrast with externals, people with a high level of internal locus are better adapted socially, have better morale and mood, have less stress and better health, and are more likely to try to improve their situation instead of passively waiting for their situation to improve. If you're an internal, however, be careful not to overestimate the scope of your responsibilities. You're not responsible for *everything*. There are some circumstances out of your control, and you can't control other people.

Here are some tips for how you can develop your internal locus of control (in other words, stop blaming others and start taking more responsibility):

1. **Remember that you always have a choice in what you feel, think, say, and do.** If you fumble and forget that you are in your driver's seat, you can regain control of the situation by choosing your emotions, reframing your thoughts, and changing your actions. Avoid seeing yourself as a victim; it's not productive, and it doesn't help anyone. Viktor Frankl, who was interned in a concentration camp during World War II, probably said it best: "Everything can be taken from a man but one thing: the last of the human freedoms – to choose one's attitude in any given set of circumstances, to choose one's own way ... When we are no longer able to change a situation, we are challenged to change ourselves ... Between stimulus and response there is a space. In that space is our power to choose our response. In our response lies our growth and our freedom."

2. **Be aware that everyone has rights AND responsibilities.** To focus solely on your rights at the expense of others' rights is an imbalanced view of the world. If you tend to say, "I have the right to ..." in situations where you feel cheated or imposed upon, or if you prefer to simply do what you feel like doing, then it might be useful to remind yourself of your responsibilities in a situation. Motivational speaker Paul Rousseau says he's tired of hearing people focus on their rights: "I am not talking here about fundamental rights, such as the right to express oneself, to vote, to be able to circulate freely, etc., but the whims which some peopleuse to avoid fulfilling

their responsibilities, whether by laziness, lack of ambition, fear, selfishness, sadness, lack of courage, and so on!" He gives plenty of examples (I have the right to let my bad temper sully the day of others; I have the right to arrive late; etc.), to which he responds: "And what is your responsibility as a leader? As a colleague? To the team?" Paul Rousseau suggests that we ask ourselves that question too, especially when we're about to say, "It's my right." When people focus on what's coming to them without thinking about how they can make a situation better, they come across as being short-sighted, reactive and selfish. Focusing on your responsibilities (the positive, respectful contribution you can make) shows that you have a broader vision of working with people.

3. **Make things happen for yourself.** Take initiative, get going with your plans, and overcome setbacks and obstacles. More often than not, successful people got that way through hard work and persistence.

4. **Take responsibility for your part of a problem, whatever it may be.** Perhaps you didn't communicate your expectations clearly, you used inflammatory words, you ignored the situation, or something else. Sure, someone may have done something wrong, but focusing on this won't move things forward.

5. **Take time to analyze the different options available when you feel stuck in a situation.** Prepare a list of the choices that you have in the situation. Then, choose the solution that shows that you are taking responsibility for yourself, while respecting your rights and those of others.

Here's your three-part challenge: In the first part of the challenge, on the first day of this week, describe in your journal a difficult situation that you experienced recently, for example, a situation in which you were in conflict with others. Analyze what you've written in terms of (a) how focused you were on your rights rather than your responsibilities in the situation, and (b) how you attributed responsibility for what happened (Whom did you blame? For what?). **Second**, become aware of your tendency to blame yourself, others, or circumstances for what's happening on a day-to-day basis. Over a period of three days this week, in your journal, keep track of each time you are blaming others; justifying your behavior, a situation, your results, and those of others; or referring to your rights. Pay attention to your conversations, emails, or thoughts, and note when you use the following words: because, because of, since, that's why, the reason being, caused by, thanks to, etc. Share your results with your feedback team, and ask them for their perceptions. **Third**, over a period of three days this week, especially when interacting with others, avoid blaming yourself, others, or circumstances for what's happening. You may do it more often than you realize. Use some of the tips above to help you find positive alternatives to the blame game. Keep track of your results in your journal.

Reflection: Answer the following questions in your journal. Regarding part 1 of the challenge, did you find this exercise challenging to carry out? Why? When you recalled the difficult event, what were your feelings and thoughts? How could you have handled this situation in a more skillful way? What would you change? Now, for each example that you noted in part 2 of the challenge, determine whether: (a) the justification concerned you personally or targeted someone else; (b) the situation was positive or negative; (c) you attributed the causes to you or something beyond your control (another person, luck, situation, etc.). Summarize your findings and look for patterns. More generally, how do you justify your situation, thoughts, and behaviors? For example, do you tend to make internal attributions for positive situations that concern you? And external attributions for negative situations that concern you? How do you usually explain the situations or behaviors of others? Do you tend to make external attributions for positive situations? Finally, regarding part 3, how often did you blame others? How challenging was it to avoid doing so? What impact did this have on your interactions?

Action Plan: What five specific actions will you take starting now to: (a) develop a stronger internal locus of control; and (b) help others do the same? Keep a record of your plan and your progress in implementing your plan in your journal.

Food for thought:

- Think about your responsibilities before claiming your rights.
- Realize that others have rights too, and that your rights aren't necessarily more important than theirs.
- Own what belongs to you. Take responsibility for yourself. Realize that you are the master of your life.

6

WHAT MOTIVATES YOU?

"It always seems impossible until it's done."
– Nelson Mandela

"If you're working on something that you really care about, you don't have to be pushed. The vision pulls you." – Steve Jobs

"What you lack in talent can be made up with desire, hustle and giving 110% all the time." – Don Zimmer

Take a few minutes to answer the following questions in your journal:

1. What makes you want to get up in the morning?
2. When is the last time you felt super motivated; in other words, willing to make a persistent, focused, and intense effort to reach a particular goal?
3. What is the last time that you felt especially unmotivated to do something? What is it about the task or the situation that may have contributed to your lack of energy?

How hard was it to answer these questions? They offer important clues about your central motivators. Everyone has a unique combination of things that energizes them. What sets awesome employees apart is that they understand what motivates them to take action, and they look for ways to motivate themselves.

For example, after having worked at an egg processing plant for four days, Sue was unable to get herself up on the fifth day. The work was dirty, smelly, routine, hard, and high pressure. Her coworkers were aggressive; they frequently "accidentally" sprayed her with a high-pressure washer while cleaning the equipment, they yelled at her, and they excluded her from their conversations during breaks. And sometimes she saw gross red spots in eggs when she was grading them. Although Sue was desperate for a summer job while going to university, she quit her job that morning. There was nothing that could make her go back to that place. She knew that this wasn't the right kind of work or workplace for her. She soon found a job working in sporting goods at Canadian Tire with a manager who valued her creativity and initiative. She watched videos about how to sell particular products such as lawn mowers and fencing, and she watched others do it. By the end of the summer, she was proud of the contribution that she made. In comparison with her day job at the egg processing plant within walking distance, at Canadian Tire, she worked split shifts, and she needed to bike an hour to and from work. Her experience that summer helped Sue understand that challenge, autonomy, and continuous learning were her central motivators, not to mention working in a respectful environment.

Can you relate to Sue's experience? This exercise will offer you some insights into your central motivators beyond the clues left by your answers to the questions at the beginning of this exercise. Be sure to do the challenge before reading any of the text that follows the drawing on the next page.

Here's your two-part challenge: In **Part 1: Without reading what's on the page after the drawing** (which might bias your answers), begin by looking at the following drawing for 10 seconds. Then, in your journal, take a full 10 minutes to write the story that you think is being depicted in the drawing. If you think you've run out of things to say, just keep writing. The more detailed your story is the better! Here are some questions to prompt your reflection:

1. What is happening in the drawing?
2. Who are the people in it?
3. What led to this situation?
4. What are the people thinking? Feeling? Doing?
5. What do they want?
6. What will happen next?

Got it? Good! This challenge is a pattern analysis exercise called the Thematic Apperception Test (TAT). The idea behind the TAT is that our motivations unconsciously infiltrate or seep into our perceptions of what's happening in a situation. The TAT is most often used in combination with David McClelland's need theory. This theory proposes that the following needs are at the heart of what motivates all actions:

1. **Achievement** – People with a high need for achievement enjoy challenges. Work goals that are too easy (or low risk) or too difficult (or high risk) are demotivating for them. Instead, they choose work goals that are moderately challenging (in other words, the goals are doable but they need to 'stretch' to attain them). They have a strong need for feedback (which can come directly from their work or from others). They enjoy either working alone in an autonomous fashion or with others who also have a strong need for achievement. They are rarely motivated by money. The opposite is true for people with a low need for achievement. Some key words used by high achievers are: success, accomplishments, competence, challenges, opportunities, personal best, feedback, autonomy, and results-driven.

2. **Affiliation** – People with a high need for affiliation enjoy working with and building relationships with others. They tend to avoid conflict situations and accommodate others' wishes even at their own expense. Compared with those with a low need for affiliation, they are more likely to conform to group norms. They prefer tasks that involve interacting with others such as working with clients. Some key words used by high affiliation folks are: getting along, building relationships, helping others, being liked, cooperation, and teamwork.

3. **Power** – There are two types of power – one good and one not so good. People with a high need for "socialized" power want to become leaders as a way of helping others and advancing the

organization's goals. However, people with a high need for "personal" power are more interested in acquiring power as a way of pursuing their own goals. Some key words used by people with a high need for "socialized" power include: influence, altruism, social responsibility, organizational goals, making a difference for others, and leadership. Some key words used by high "personal" power folks are: control, status, prestige, personal advancement, authority, competing, discipline, material wealth, and winning.

To varying degrees, we all need achievement, belonging, and power. However, usually, one of these needs is a particularly strong motivator that influences our behavior across many situations. Knowing what motivates you will help you find a job and work environment that fits your most important needs and, as a result, feels natural and enjoyable for you. Knowing your central motivators will help you put yourself in situations where you'll be getting your most important needs met. And, as we saw with Sue, it might also help you make the tough decision to leave a job that drains you of energy.

You might wonder what kind of central motivators leaders have. According to David McClelland, people with a high need for achievement can be great entrepreneurs but they're often too independent to be great team leaders. Similarly, those with a high need for affiliation may find it difficult to make challenging people-related decisions. And those with a high need for personal power can be manipulative and overly self-interested. The best leaders are those who have: (a) a high need for social power (they want to achieve the goals of the organization and help others); (b) a weak need for personal power (they don't see power as a prestige symbol or as a way of advancing their own interests); (c) a moderately high need for achievement (but not too much!); and (d) a low need for belonging (the need for social approval makes difficult decisions even more difficult, but some need for affiliation is still required).

Are you wondering how well money works as motivator? For some people, money appears to be a central motivator; that is, until you ask them if they would be willing to do "anything" to earn lots of money. At the same time, most people want to be fairly paid while doing work that meets their needs. Bill George and his colleagues found that most leaders realize that truly meaningful success involves pursuing intrinsic motivations such as challenge, contribution, having a positive impact, and making a difference in the lives of others. Continuing to chase after external markers of success such as recognition, money, prestige, and possessions is an exercise in futility. No matter how successful you become, the goal posts always change; you'll always think that you can be more successful, richer, better recognized, etc. As a result, you're always striving and never arriving at your destination.

Are you ready to look for patterns in the story that you wrote in Part 1? If so, move on to Part 2.

Part 2: Review the descriptions of the three motivators, read your story, and interpret what it says about your central motivators. For example, if your story is full of words related to challenge, success, and autonomy, then accomplishment is likely your central motivator. If your story's focus is on the relationship between the two individuals, their friendship, and teamwork, then affiliation is likely an important motivator for you. Finally, if your story is about the power of one person over another or even the ability of a person to make a difference in the world, then power is a central motivator. If you have an electronic copy of your story, you can also copy and paste it at the University of Texas at Austin's online TAT (www.utpsyc.org/TATintro/). Aside from helping you interpret your story, this site will provide you with loads of interesting information. Next, without telling them about your own interpretation, read your story to your feedback team, and ask them to determine its primary themes and to what degree each of the three needs motivates you. Keep track of your and your feedback team's interpretations in your journal.

Reflection: Answer the following questions in your journal.

1. **What does your story say about what motivates you?** How do your answers fit: (a) your expectations of your key motivational factors and (b) your answers to the opening questions? When you think back to the three most significant moments in your life, what themes that stand out? How are they related to your central motivators?

2. **Imagine that you have your dream job.** Describe it in as much detail as possible in your journal. What would that job look like? What would you be doing? Who would you be working with? Review what you've written, and examine the role that your central motivators play in your ideal job. If they are important motivators, they should be obvious. Are there other factors involved? For example, do you want a job that involves a variety of tasks, requires a diversity of skills, is central to the organization's mission, allows you to work autonomously and make decisions about how you get your work done, and offers you clear feedback? According to the job characteristics theory developed by economist Greg Oldham and psychologist Richard Hackman, jobs with these features tend to motivate people. Which of these features would motivate YOU?

3. Beyond impacting your view of your dream job, **your central motivators also influence your view of an ideal organization.** In your journal, take a few minutes to describe your ideal organization. What leadership style is used? How is success measured (if at all)? What is the importance of results vs. relationships? Flexibility vs. control? Stability vs. change? How much emphasis is there on competition? Based on their ground-breaking research, business professors Kim Cameron

and Robert Quinn identified four kinds of organizational cultures:

a. **Clan/family** (Let's collaborate!) – focus on relationships, mentoring, teamwork, cohesion, participation, flexibility, commitment, and collaboration. Example: Tom's of Maine

b. **Innovation/entrepreneurial** (Let's create!) – focus on adapting, creativity, individual freedom, change, risk-taking, and networking. Examples: Facebook, Google, Adobe

c. **Hierarchy/formal** (Let's control!) – focus on structure, standardize, stability, coordination, predictability, efficiency, and analysis. Examples: McDonalds, government organizations

d. **Market/competitive** (Let's compete!) – focus on results-oriented, goal-oriented, profitability, and strategizing. Example: General Electric

Which of these four organizational cultures appeal to you? In which type of organization do you think you are most likely to find your dream job? Just like your dream job, your ideal organization will fit with your central motivators. For example, if creativity and autonomy are part of your central motivators, a job in which you're closely supervised in an organization that rewards conformity and obedience to rules will feel demotivating. If there's a poor fit between your ideal organization and the one you work for, you'll likely feel frustrated, stressed, less interested in your work, and out of tune with others. Certainly, your performance would suffer and your career options in the organization would be limited. You'll feel like a round peg in a square hole! In contrast, finding your dream job in your ideal organization will help you feel right at home and motivated to do your work.

Action Plan: Describe the three specific actions you will take starting now to increase your personal motivation. David McClelland's extensive international research points to the importance of developing your need for achievement in creating personal and professional success. What three actions will you take starting now to increase your sense of achievement? Keep a record of your plan and your progress in implementing your plan in your journal.

Food for thought:

- Look for a job and workplace where you can use and be appreciated for your key strengths and your central motivators. If you choose a job based solely on which pays the best, you may find it hard to wake up in the morning!
- Know where you want to go in life and how to get there. The alternative is to aimlessly drift through life and, before you know it, 20 years have passed by!
- Motivate yourself. Be a self-starter; don't wait for others or the right circumstances to motivate you. Remember that you are the CEO of You Incorporated.

PART 2: MANAGING YOURSELF

7

HOW WELL DO YOU MANAGE YOURSELF?

"No man is free who is not master of himself." – Epictetus

"The first and best victory is to conquer self." – Plato

"Discipline equals freedom." – Jocko Williams & Leif Babin

"We cannot become what we need to be
by remaining what we are." – Max DePree

This is your life. Grab it by the helm. – Unknown Source

On a scale of 1 to 10, how good are you at managing yourself? How self-disciplined are you? Do you have constructive thoughts and behaviors 100% of the time? Or do you slip up some of the time, finding it challenging to work through difficult situations? Awesome employees make an effort to manage themselves. They are responsible, self-aware, self-controlled, self-motivated, and able to work on their own without constant guidance. People who don't manage themselves are like a boat without a rudder! They let the wind (others) determine their direction and speed.

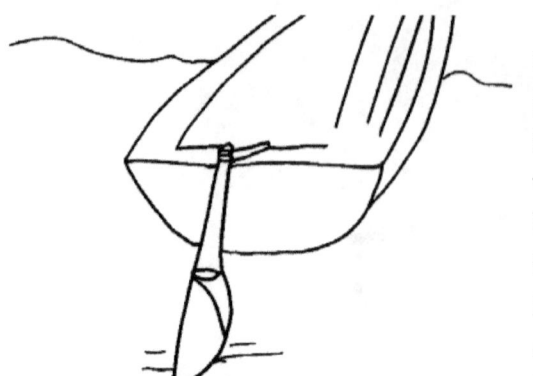

The idea of self-management (and later, self-leadership) started many years ago with the ground-breaking work of Charles Manz and Henry Sims. They considered self-leadership to be a type of substitute for leadership: if employees are able to manage themselves, then there isn't much need for someone else to prod, control, or steer them in the right direction. Self-leadership has three elements:

1. **Developing constructive, optimistic thoughts.** This involves replacing dysfunctional thought patterns with positive self-talk and mental imagery.

2. **Managing your actions through self-awareness and self-evaluation.** This involves observing yourself and identifying behaviors that need to be modified, setting goals that guide your future efforts, developing rewards that motivate you to meet your goals, and giving yourself feedback that steers any unproductive behavior in more positive directions.

3. **Creating natural reward strategies** by looking for the intrinsically enjoyable aspects of tasks.

How do you think you stack up? Is self-leadership something that you actively pursue, or do you find yourself being passive, waiting for direction, inspiration, and motivation from someone else? Do you postpone important tasks to the point where you're rushing to complete them at the last minute? Do you delay gratification and resist temptations? When you're unmotivated, how do you deal with it? What do you do, if anything, to transform a sense of disinterest and indifference into enthusiasm and engagement? What do you do to take charge of your "boat" and steer it toward success? As Jocko Williams and Leif Babin argue in their bestseller *Extreme Ownership*, "The test is not a complex one: when the alarm goes off, do you get up out of bed, or do you lie there in comfort and fall back to sleep? If you have the discipline to get out of bed, you win – you pass the test. If you are mentally weak for that moment and you let that weakness keep you in bed, you fail. Though it seems small, that weakness translates to more significant decisions. But if you exercise discipline, that too translates to more substantial elements of your life."

Jocko Williams and Leif Babin's message may sound harsh, but it echoes Walter Mischel's research findings. In his book *Emotional Intelligence*, Daniel Goleman presents the scenario that Walter Mischel used in many studies: "Imagine that you're four years old and someone makes you the following proposition: Here's a marshmallow. You can eat it whenever you want. But, if you wait for a few minutes, I'll give you two marshmallows as a reward." What would you most likely do? (If eating a marshmallow doesn't tempt you, replace it with something more tempting for you.) Would you wait for the researcher to return, or would you swallow the marshmallow as soon as the researcher leaves the room?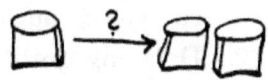

The long-term results of Walter Mischel's studies are revealing. Children who ate the marshmallow immediately became adults who were less confident and less in control of themselves as well as more impulsive. As adults, those who had been able to wait patiently for the two marshmallows were more confident and more able to deal with stress and reach their goals. It's interesting how such a simple experiment can predict success in life.

What distinguished these two groups of children was whether they used their "hot" (emotional, reactive) system or their "cool" (thoughts, reflection) system to control their impulses. When the children focused on "cool" aspects of the rewards (thinking about marshmallows as clouds), they were able to wait much longer than those who focused on the "warm" aspects of the rewards (thinking about the sweet and chewy marshmallows). The researchers concluded that, "People have the power to create the mental conditions that can help them resist temptation and cope with adversity. Effective self-control requires one to be strategic in knowing when to 'cool' and when to 'warm,' taking into account characteristics of each situation." They also found that self-distraction served as a good way of increasing self-control. During the experiment, for example, when the children were asked to think about "mommy pushing them on a swing" or when they were distracted with an activity, delay time was much longer than those who were told to think about the marshmallows.

Here are some of key elements of self-management and self-discipline:
1. **Working through challenging situations** by managing what you say to yourself and taking positive, constructive actions.
2. **Delaying gratification.** This means being able to hold off on doing things that you feel like doing in exchange for bigger rewards later on; in other words, trading short-term and short-lived satisfaction for the achievement of longer term goals.
3. **Tolerating frustration**. This involves persevering in the face of competing demands. For example, someone who slams on his horn and screams insults at other drivers in a traffic jam doesn't tolerate frustration well.
4. **Thinking before speaking or acting.** People who think before speaking are less likely to regret what they say. Ask yourself if your comments are essential or if you can keep your

remark to yourself. You may need to take a deep breath and count to 10 or ask the person to give you some time to think about things.

5. **Putting things into perspective.** Some things that seem important right now become completely unimportant in the long term. Ask yourself, "Will this be important in 10 years?" Beyond that, there are things that we can control and act on and things that we can't control and shouldn't act on. As you can see on the following personal power grid developed by burnout researchers Dennis Jaffee and Cynthia Scott, there are two continuums: how much control we have in a situation versus how to respond in the situation.

	Can be Controlled	Risk Zone	Can't be Controlled
Take Action	Situation Mastery		Ceaseless Striving
Don't Act	Giving Up		Letting Go

According to Dennis Jaffee and Cynthia Scott, taking action is appropriate only when you can control a situation. This is an example of situation mastery. You engage in ceaseless striving when you try to take action over things that you can't control. For example, this might occur when you're trying to change someone else's behavior. They must want to change their behavior for change to happen in the relationship. You are giving up when you don't take action over things that you can control. This might happen when you allow others to make decisions for you, when you feel helpless or hopeless in a situation, or when you simply conform to popular opinion rather than take risks. The flipside of situation mastery is letting go, which is appropriate when you don't have control and you don't take action. This is an especially difficult but important skill to learn. As you can imagine, the best use of your energy is spending time in situation mastery and letting go.

If you're having trouble letting go, the following rules may be helpful: "Rule 1. Don't sweat the small stuff. Rule 2. It's all small stuff. Rule 3. If you can't fight or flee, then flow" (author unknown).

Rule 1: Don't sweat the small stuff: You may need to prioritize and identify the things that are worth worrying about and worry about those – but not excessively. Worry doesn't improve situations; constructive problem solving does! Get some perspective on what's important and remember not to let the small stuff get to you.

Rule 2: It's all small stuff: Take care of yourself, keep things in perspective and let go of anxiety. If you don't have your health, it doesn't matter how many important things you think you have to do, they won't get accomplished. Nothing is worth compromising your health when it comes right down to it.

Rule 3: If you can't fight or flee, flow: When it's worth the fight (for example, it's something that will have a huge impact on you and/or others), you should take some kind of action (not necessarily fighting, though!). But if you shouldn't or can't fight, and can't flee or run away to release energy, then simply let it be and flow. Go with the flow, not against the current.

In any situation, try to find the part over which you have some control even when you think you have no control. Venture out of any limiting beliefs you have, and try new things within your risk zone (things that are only somewhat within your control). Here's an example: Sue is at the airport, and she just heard that her flight is delayed two hours due to weather conditions. Sue doesn't take out her frustration on others. She tries to let go and shift her focus from feeling frustrated to accepting that she can't control the weather and nor can anyone else. She takes a few deep breaths, calls people awaiting her arrival at her destination, goes for a walk, talks with other stranded passengers, and reads a new book that she brought along.

Here's your two-part challenge: In **part 1**, think about a time when you experienced a significant stressful or negative experience in your life. What did you say to yourself during this experience? In other words, what were your thoughts about the situation, yourself, and others who may have been involved? How did you feel in the situation? Describe specific emotions that you were experiencing. What did you do to deal with the experience? Describe your actions and reactions. Keep track of your story and your analysis of it in your journal.

In **part 2,** you'll explore your capacity to engage in self-discipline. Spend a few minutes identifying your most important priorities and goals for a three-day period this week. Identify the five most important things that are likely to distract you and how you can reduce their impact. Then, during this time period, try to focus on your priorities and goals. Avoid distractions and doing things that will take your focus away from your priorities and goals. Delay gratification, tolerate frustration, think before speaking or doing something, and put things in perspective. Stay in the healthiest quadrants of the personal power grid: mastering the situation and letting go. For example, if you are caught in the "incessant effort" quadrant, ask yourself what you could do to move to the "letting go" quadrant. Keep track of your challenges and successes in your journal.

Reflection: Answer the following questions in your journal. Regarding part 1, what did you learn about yourself in this experience? What does your experience say about your ability to manage yourself? Now, were you to re-live this stressful experience, what could you say to yourself that would be more empowering and constructive? How would you prefer to feel in the experience? What thoughts might help you transform negative emotions in positive or neutral emotions? What can you do differently that would help you to be more personally effective in dealing with the situation? Regarding part 2, what were your reactions during the exercise? Was the exercise easy or difficult to do? Why? What do your actions say about your ability to engage in self-discipline? What personal habits have you developed to help you be more disciplined?

Action Plan: What five specific actions will you take starting now to exercise more self-management and self-discipline? Keep a record of your plan and your progress in implementing your plan in your journal.

Food for thought:

- Manage yourself. Don't wait for your secret prince(ss) to come along and rescue you from your situation. If you're not happy, do something about it. Don't make others unhappy by whining about it. Figure out what you can do to fix a situation.
- Wait for the second marshmallow! Delay gratification, put things in perspective, think before speaking, and do all the great things associated with emotionally intelligent people.
- Focus on what matters most to you.
- Remember that you are the captain of your ship. You get to steer the rudder. Don't get bogged down by trivialities.
- If you feel overwhelmed by a situation, don't react to it immediately. Give yourself time to reflect, call a friend, and put it in perspective.

8

ARE YOU GUILTY OF STINKING THINKING?

"The biggest obstacle to solving our own problems
is that we frequently confuse reality with what we make up."
– Miles Sherts

"Don't attribute to malice that which can be explained otherwise."
– Alain de Botton

"What disturbs men's minds is not events
but their judgements of events." – Epictetus

Do you think that you're totally clear-minded and objective when you're evaluating a situation, yourself, or someone else? Or are you boxing yourself or others in with your stinking thinking? Have you ever been in a situation in which your perception or thoughts about the situation or the other person weren't warranted? When you realized that you jumped the gun? Usually, this means that perceptual errors and cognitive distortions have seeped into how you see and interpret things. Because we're bombarded by loads of information, our brains take shortcuts and pay attention to only some of that information. Although this speeds up how we process that the world around us, it also results in errors. Combine these perceptual errors with cognitive distortions, which are irrational thought patterns that interfere with how we perceive the world around us (according to David Burns), and we have a recipe for disaster.

There are many causes of perceptual errors and cognitive distortions, but they all boil down to not taking the time to think something through and do a reality check. For example, Bob might rush to a judgement about Coco without taking the time to develop a more complete picture of who she is. Or Coco may dislike people who wear orange and automatically conclude that they're 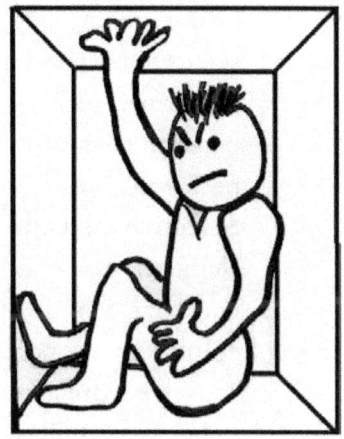 incompetent. She bases her judgement of people on something entirely irrelevant. Or Sue expects that her new supervisor will be demanding and, lo and behold, he is demanding. We're often not aware of our errors and distortions, and even awesome employees are subject to them. How they deal with them is what sets them apart from the rest of the pack. Awesome employees take time to gather information about a person or situation, use all this information to arrive at a conclusion, and challenge any limiting perceptions, thoughts, and beliefs that they have about people. They don't stay in the box too long!

Below is a list of 10 common perceptual errors and cognitive distortions. As you read the list, check off the ones that you're most likely to engage in. Also, try to find personal examples for each error and distortion. This could be something that you did or that someone else did.

1. **First impressions:** Involves forming an idea about a person or situation based on our first impression, and then only paying attention to subsequent information that confirms our first impression. For example, if you think that Bob has a great sense of humor when you meet him, as you get to know him, you'll especially notice his sense of humor.

2. **Contrast effect:** Involves evaluating a person or situation relative to another. For example, Coco, an average performer, seems to be a poor performer when she's contrasted with a high performer such as Sue; or Coco may come across as a high performer when she's compared to an especially poor performer.

3. **Selective perception:** Involves paying attention only to the elements that confirm our existing opinions. For example, if you have a poor opinion of Coco, you will only notice what confirms your perception and ignore any of Coco's strengths. This perceptual error overlaps with the cognition distortion called mental filter. When Sue is doing positive mental filtering in relation to her job, she ignores all the negative aspects of the job. When she's doing negative mental filtering, all she sees are the bad things about her job.

4. **Halo/horns effect or labeling:** Involves allowing a single characteristic of a person to influence our overall opinion of that person (whether positive or negative). For example, Bob might think that Sue's an overall awesome employee just because she says hello to him as she walks by his office in the morning. As an example of the horns effect, Bob may think that his supervisor is a tyrant if his supervisor happened to scold him once for using his cellphone during a meeting.

5. **Projection:** Involves transferring our feelings and preoccupations to another person. For example, Sue might tell others that they look worried, when, in reality, it is Sue that is worried.

6. **Stereotyping or clichés:** Involves reducing our perceptions of a situation or a person to categories conveyed in society. For example, Bob may think that Coco drives poorly because she's a woman or that Sue is "cultured" because her family is from France.

7. **All or nothing thinking:** Involves thinking in extremes. Things are all black or white; there aren't any shades of grey. For example, Bob expected to achieve 100% of his sales target, but he achieves only 90% of it, and he feels like a failure.

8. **Generalization:** Involves making broad claims based on a few examples. For example, thinking that certain things always happen to you or that other things never happen to you based on a few experiences. For example, Sue missed the bus this morning and concluded that this always happens to her. Or, Sue saw Coco bringing work home one day and concluded that Coco always brings her work home. In the same way, people can be prone to exaggeration and minimization. For example, Bob might overestimate the impact of his weaknesses (thinking that they will prevent him from having any kind of career) and, at the same time, minimize the importance of his many talents.

9. **Jumping to hasty conclusions or making undue interpretations:** Involves drawing conclusions without taking the time to verify our interpretation and collect more facts. For example, Coco thinks that Sue hates her because Sue pressed the "close door" button of the elevator just as she was arriving (in reality, Sue meant to press the "open door" button but got mixed up).

10. **Emotional Reasoning:** Involves thinking that your emotional reaction to a situation reflects the truth or the reality of the situation (regardless of the facts of the situation). Sue might feel angry with Bob and, as a result, conclude that he did something wrong.

Have you been able to identify the errors and biases that are most likely to color your view of the world? As you can imagine, walking around unaware of them can have a nasty effect on your ability to see the world as it is. Your communications, relationships, and productivity are all likely to suffer as a result of them. So how can you avoid these errors and distortions?

1. **Become aware of them.** We tend to function in autopilot and be unaware of our biases and errors. Aside from stopping to think about what you're doing, it may help to ask others for their perceptions.

2. **Obtain concrete and objective facts about the situation.** Separate the facts from your interpretations which are often laced with errors and biases. Describe the situation that triggered your error or distortion. In doing so, you will be obliged to relate facts, not your interpretation of these facts. Ask yourself what evidence would be needed to support your point of view, and try to see if this evidence exists. Maybe you will see that the situation is not negative after all or that you overreacted. Don't rush to conclusions; take your time.

3. **Try to see the situation from a variety of perspectives.** This may include neutral observers or the other person involved in a situation. Put yourself in the other person's shoes and try to understand the situation from their point of view, but also get feedback from others. Leave room for alternative hypotheses. Give people the benefit of the doubt. Don't presume that they are out to get you. Pay attention to any of your behaviors that might influence the behavior of others. For example, Coco is being aloof toward Bob because she feels that he is ignoring her. Now, Bob is being reserved toward Coco because he doesn't understand why her behavior has changed. Coco should realize that Bob's behavior toward her is influenced by her behavior toward him.

4. **Pay attention to any factors or context that might influence the situation** and that may be beyond everyone's control. Eliminate other potential explanations before blaming the situation on others. The number of errors and distortions that we make increase significantly when situations are unexpected, complex, or unclear and when we're not sure how to deal with them.

5. **Avoid making arbitrary and categorical judgments.** Leave room for alternative explanations. Often, by saying what you think out loud, you will find that it is farfetched or inappropriate. Moreover, do not draw hasty conclusions; ask yourself if what you think would make sense to an objective observer. For example, despite his overall good attendance record, Bob arrives late twice in the same week. If Sue bases her perception solely on Bob's behaviors this week, she will say that he tends to be tardy and disorganized.

6. **Remind yourself that you don't perceive things as they really are (and neither do others).** On the contrary, information is selected, organized, and interpreted by our brains to satisfy our needs and confirm our attitudes. The perceived world is not the real world. Give people the benefit of the doubt.

7. **Remind yourself that situations are neutral, and that it's your interpretation of the situation that creates problems for you.** Recognize that errors and distortions arise from thoughts you have about a situation and that they do not represent the situation itself. The situation itself is neutral. It becomes positive or negative depending on the label you put on it. So, don't take everything personally, and don't assume that someone intends to attack you or insult you.

8. **Try to perceive things accurately.** Each of us has a personal frame of reference which filters all sensory data that we receive (what we see, hear, feel, smell, and taste). This frame of

reference is influenced by several factors such as our needs, our past experiences, our self-esteem, and our personal traits. In judging another person, you might ask, "Is my frame of reference clouding my vision of the 'real' person and how he's behaving right now?" Try to become aware of what is in your "box" and limiting your perspective of the situation. In addition, try to set aside your own frame of reference in order to grasp the other person's frame.

9. **Stop worrying about what might happen.** If you are feeling stressed, your perceptions and thoughts will be especially distorted. Take a break to calm down and breathe if you feel particularly stressed or upset. When you're calm and relaxed, you'll be in a better position to deal with a situation.

10. **Identify fair and balanced thoughts.** For example, instead of seeing everything in black and white (I'm either stupid or I'm amazing), try to be more nuanced (I'm very good, but I should work at certain things to get even better). Challenge your errors and distortions and replace them with realistic thoughts.

11. **Think about what you could do about the situation.** By having a more balanced perspective, the situation may stop being important and you may decide that you don't need to take special steps to resolve it. Realize that most things that people worry about don't happen.

12. **Create positive affirmations** that you can use to counter errors and distortions in the future. For example, instead of saying "I'm incompetent," say "I'm still learning."

13. **Take responsibility for yourself.** If what you say is peppered with excuses, look for patterns in the types of excuses you make and find alternatives to them.

Here is your two-part challenge: In **part 1,** at the end of three days this week, read the descriptions of perceptual errors and cognitive distortions. Identify those that reflect the ways of thinking you used and reactions you had during the day. Then, find counter-arguments that will enable you to have a more accurate perception of what you are experiencing. Identify objective evidence or facts that: (a) support your errors and distortions; and (b) contradict them. You might create the following chart in your journal.

Situation	Example : On arriving at work...
Thoughts	I have too much work. I'll never finish it. My day is ruined!
Type of error or distortion	Hasty conclusion
Emotions and behaviors	Panic; discouragement; anxiety; inability to concentrate
Alternative thoughts	I can ask for help. I can prioritize my work. I usually manage to get lots done. I'm an efficient worker.

In **part 2**, review and follow the tips for identifying and controlling your biases and distortions during the following four days of the week. Keep track of your efforts in your journal.

Reflection: Answer the following questions in your journal. How did you feel during this exercise? How challenging was it to pay attention to your perceptual errors and cognitive distortions? What are the three errors and distortions that you made most often? When and why do you think you made them? What attempts did you make to eliminate them? How successful were your attempts? What lessons have you learned in doing this exercise?

Action Plan: Describe three steps that you will take from now on to recognize and remove the cognitive distortions and perceptual errors from your impulses. Be creative! Keep a record of your plan and your progress in implementing your plan in your journal.

Food for thought:

- Realize that not everyone sees and interprets a situation in the same way that you do. In the same image, you might see two faces, someone else might see a vase. Don't insist that your interpretations are correct and others' are wrong. Be open to other interpretations.
- Avoid perceptual errors and cognitive biases as often as you can. We all make them, so don't be too hard on yourself. Try to be more conscious of them, and check the accuracy of your perceptions.
- Challenge your stinking thinking with positive, affirming thoughts that make life better for you and others.
- Don't ass│u│me. Check your perceptions. Ask yourself, "Did I understand this correctly, or is there something that I'm missing? Am I seeing the situation though 'mud colored' glasses due to stress, hunger, fatigue, or other factors?"

9
....

ARE YOU MANAGING YOUR ATTITUDES AND EMOTIONS?

"The cure for boredom is curiosity.
There is no cure for curiosity." – Dorothy Parker

"What happens is not as important as
how you react to what happens." – Thaddeus Golas

"People are hired for their aptitude,
but fired for their attitude." – Chantal Binet

How would you react to a flat tire? In his classic book *The Sky is the Limit*, motivational guru Wayne Dyer presents the following situation. Imagine that you're driving along a deserted highway at 3 a.m. one summer night. You're alone with no cellphone, OnStar, or ability to contact another person. You run over a nail in the road, and your car gets a flat tire. Although you have a spare tire in the trunk, you've never changed a tire in your life. Before reading any further, try to imagine what you would do in this situation.

Now, read the following five scenarios and identify the ones that most closely resemble what you would do in the situation:

1. **You feel panicky!** You have a big problem, and you're at a loss to resolve it. You start crying or yelling. You get out of your car, look at the tire, and then kick your tire or the nail on the road. You're afraid that you'll be stuck forever, that robbers might come along, or  a bear, or … any number of scenarios might unfold, but all of them nasty. Instead of focusing on solving the problem, you spend your time being anxious, angry, frustrated, and confused. Thoughts of the worst case scenario consume your mind, and you flail about aimlessly. "Why does this always happen to me?"

2. **You're stuck in inertia.** You can't believe what just happened, and you just sit there, frozen. You're unable to move yourself and do something. You lament your bad luck, regretting your being there in the first place and blaming whatever or whomever caused you to be in these circumstances. You feel stuck, hopeless, and helpless. "There's nothing I can do about it, so why fight it?" you say to yourself, while resigning yourself to the situation. "I can't believe this really happen to me."

3. **You strive to deal with the situation.** You open the trunk, move all the stuff that you stockpile in your trunk out of the way, and pull out the spare tire and the jack. But then you realize that you don't know how to work the jack or take a tire off. You walk half a mile looking for a house or a gas station, but then you turn back because you don't see any buildings. Besides, walking in the dark isn't your cup of tea! You go back to the car. Maybe you fall into panic or inertia. Or, you carry the jack and the spare tire toward the flat tire and try to figure out what to do, but you give up because it's too confusing. And you might

screw up. You think about blowing your horn or driving your car slowly. You struggle to find a solution, and you're going from one idea to the next, but success eludes you. Survival is your aim. "What should I do? What should I do? What…."

4. **You cope with the situation**. Knowing that being frozen in fear or being overly anxious about a situation aren't effective, you decide to simply adjust to it. You try to stay calm and understand your situation: "It's 3 a.m., no one's likely to come around, and I didn't see any houses on my way here. I should at least try to install the spare tire myself." Or you decide that, realistically, you wouldn't be able to install the spare tire in the dark, so you switch on the flashers, and get ready to sleep in your car. You may be able to flag someone down in the morning. Whatever you decide, it'll fit with what is expected of you and what you expect of yourself given your background and experience level. You simply try to face the problem as best you can. Doing what can be expected is your motto. "Realistically, what can I do to help myself?"

5. **You are the master of your fate.** Even if you have zero experience changing a tire, you don't let this stop you. You're confident in your ability to confront challenges head-on. In fact, you love challenges because although you might make some mistakes, you might also learn something new that will be useful in the future. Besides, challenges can be exciting adventures! You find the owner's manual, the jack and the spare tire, and you start changing the tire. You take a deep breath, look at the stars in the sky, and enjoy the serenity of the night. Your focus is on being your best self and being totally engaged in the present moment. "Ah, life is good!"

Which scenarios did you choose? Which best represent how you normally deal with problems or issues? Do you typically start by being mad and swearing (scenario 1), but then quickly move on to cope with the situation (scenario 4)? According to Wayne Dyer, **our behavior in this situation echoes how we tend to deal with life's challenges more generally.** You can't control whether or not you have a flat tire, but you can control your reaction to it. Lots of people spend time in scenarios 1 and 2 when they have given up trying to change a situation. The strivers (scenario 3) struggle to handle day-to-day challenges, but don't improve their situation very much. According to Wayne Dyer, most people consider coping (scenario 4) to be the ideal solution; in other words, that well-adjusted people simply try to adapt to the situation. But, he equates this with conforming to societal expectations ("trying to be normal") rather than being the master of yourself. Wayne Dyer argues that mastery over oneself (scenario 5) is where we should hang our hat. If we are masters of ourselves, we're in the driver's seat of our own cars (flat tire or not!). According to him, "Mastery means being master of your own fate – being the one person who decides how you are going to live, react and feel in virtually every situation that life presents to you ... It is about going after what you really want and feel inside yourself, instead of hanging on to the familiar or routine and staying at those lower rungs on the ladder. It is about trusting yourself and taking risks."

Every day, from the moment we wake up, we are faced with thousands of choices. Some of these choices are small such as opening your eyes. Some are automatic; we just follow our routines, for example, brushing our teeth. Some require more deliberate thought and energy, such as what task you will handle first. Every day, we choose, sometimes without thinking, how to spend our money, where to invest our time, how we'll treat others, and whether we'll have a good day or not. The weight of all of these choices add up over time and become who we are; in other words, we become our choices. And we can change our choices as we become aware of them.

As Wayne Dyer suggests, we can even choose and control our feelings and thoughts. Awesome employees know this. They choose to adopt positive and constructive attitudes because they know they can, and they know that this allows them to be proactive rather than reactive.

One of our choices is whether we are happy or not. There's lots of research that points to the **benefits of expressing positive emotions**. People who tend to have negative emotions (such as anger, frustration, anxiety, or jealousy) tend to experience more distress, agitation, and insecurity and less engagement. They're more reactive and easily stressed. Not fun to be around! In contrast, those who tend to express positive emotions (happiness, gratitude, optimism) have higher levels of energy and motivation, better concentration, resilience, and overall health. They are also magnets for opportunities. When leaders express positive emotions, their teams have higher performance levels and lower turnover levels, according to researchers Jennifer George and Kenneth Bettenhausen. Paul Harvey, Jason Stoner, Wayne Hochwarter, and Charles Kacmar found that the opposite is also true: teams with leaders who express negative emotions have low performance levels and higher turnover. Other research by Dean McKay on "depressed interactions" shows that employees who interact with unhappy individuals as part of their work end up not only absorbing the unhappiness but also feeling hostile and anxious. Not only is negativity highly contagious, but people don't care to interact with negative people and think less of them. Would you rather be surrounded by people who have morose, self-victimizing attitudes or people who are optimistic and collaborative? Taken together, this points to the importance of being positive and upbeat at work.

A good first step is connecting with what you're feeling; in other words, being able to identify the precise emotion that you're feeling (not simply saying that you feel good or bad). It's useful to see your emotions as information, in other words, as a signal that something is or isn't working well for you.

As Eckhart Tolle once said: "The main cause of misfortune is never the situation, but your thoughts about it. Be aware of your thoughts. Separate them from the situation, which is always neutral, and always as it is. There is the situation or the facts, here is my reflection on this subject. Instead of inventing stories, stay on the facts." *Stories* are our interpretations of things; they are what cause us to feel bad. Whenever you have difficulty managing your moods or moving beyond your feelings of frustration, anger, or annoyance, you may find it helpful to ask yourself five questions:

- What are the objective facts of the situation? This is especially helpful for putting things in perspective if you tend to make a mountain out of a molehill. If you're having trouble separating your interpretations from the facts, try to look at the situation from the perspective of a third person. What would someone witnessing the situation observe?

- How do I feel? What am I thinking? These are your interpretations and reactions to the situation.

- What would I like to feel? Because it's easy to get stuck in a whirlwind of negativity, and concentrate on the negative, we need to ask ourselves what we want in a situation.

- What can I do to feel better about the situation? This step puts the control in your hands. Rather than sinking in quicksand of your own making, you can take steps toward self-mastery.

For example, at a recent team meeting on the topic of the annual summer BBQ, Sue was feeling annoyed that no one was asking her for her opinion. She began to think that no one appreciated what she might have to say, and she considered leaving the meeting. She wanted to feel valued and included, not left out. But, during a lull in the discussion, Sue decided to share her idea that represented a compromise among all the options that had been suggested. The team's attention turned to her suggestion, and Sue felt much more involved in the meeting. She realized that to feel included, she needed to include herself.

Here's another example: One morning, Bob arrived at work in a bad mood – annoyed, hassled, and overwhelmed. Things didn't go well at the office the previous day, there was a traffic jam, and he hadn't slept well. He was in no mood to make the presentation that was scheduled in an hour. Bob closed the door of his office, took a few deep breathes, relaxed, and asked himself what emotions and attitudes would help him make a great presentation. Enthusiasm. Positivity. Wanting to connect with others. Bob thought about times when he felt enthusiastic and positive and when he felt that he had really connected with others. He looked over his notes for the presentation, put a smile on his face, and left for his presentation. He felt in control and eager to make the presentation.

In both examples, Sue and Bob took some time to reflect on what they were feeling and thinking. It can be hard to realize that you have the power to lift yourself out of whatever gloomy mood you may be feeling. Sometimes, you might just feel like soaking in your misery, saying that you were wronged and you have a right to be negative. But if you spend lots of time blaming others and feeling victimized, you're giving them power to control you. Aside from your initial emotional reactions, your emotions and attitudes are under your control. Take charge of them, and you take charge of yourself.

Sue and Bob recognized that they needed to do something different to make the situation work for them. Instead of continuing to brood about not being involved, Sue decided to involve herself. Bob recognized that his mood wouldn't help him, so he figured out what would be helpful, and he did it. Sue's decision to take responsibility for her own experience and Bob's mood management both had positive results. We can follow their example.

Here's your two-part challenge: The discussion above pointed out the need to recognize what triggers our negativity and manage the difficult moments as they arise so that we can achieve mastery over ourselves. In addition, according to prolific author John Maxwell, we need to reflect on and deal with our attitudinal and emotional habits and patterns. In **part 1**, you will inventory and "clean up" habits that may be blocking your progression up the mastery ladder. As proposed by John Maxwell, ask yourself:

1. What negative emotions do I frequently have that I have trouble managing? For example, fear, frustration, jealousy, sadness, doubt, or anger.
2. What attitudes or thinking patterns tend to get me in trouble? For example, fearing the worst, expecting others to read my mind, feeling incompetent, automatically interpreting what others say as an attack.
3. Which of my behaviors are especially ineffective? For example, being passive, not saying what's on my mind, waiting until the last minute, reacting quickly, criticizing, and nitpicking.

Next, identify helpful ways of thinking, for example:

1. Transform the negative emotions into positive ones. For example, identifying thoughts that can help you feel happy, confident, empathetic, and accepting.
2. Challenge and replace negative attitudes with positive ones. For example, thoughts such as: I can do this, I will ask for what I want, I am a competent person, I'm still learning how to __ so I can ask for help, I will think the best and ask for clarification.
3. Substitute ineffective behaviors with positive ones. For example, thoughts that would encourage you to: be proactive, say what's on your mind in a respectful manner, plan your work, reflect before reacting, appreciate rather than criticize.

By now, you should have three lists of things you can say to yourself that would yield positive emotions and thoughts and constructive behaviors and bring you closer to mastery. Look for patterns in your lists and try to identify the four or five things you can say to yourself that turn the positivity switch on for your emotions, thoughts, and behaviors. Now, share your answers to the questions, your lists, and your final five positive messages with your feedback team. Ask for their feedback, and modify your work as you see fit. Develop a plan with your feedback team that describes how they will support and encourage you to maintain positive attitudes and emotions and warn you if you get off track. Keep a record of your efforts in your journal.

In **part 2**, you will test the effectiveness of your five positive messages in helping you to experience a sense of mastery. For at least three days this week, show only positive emotions and attitudes. Avoid talking about negative things, sharing or listening to gossip, and expressing negative attitudes. Try to control your emotions so that they serve you instead of hurting you. Before you react, stop and think. Change your perspective. Give people the benefit of the doubt. When negative emotions arise (for example, frustration, anger, sadness, anxiety, boredom, or irritation), ask yourself if this emotion helps or hinders you. If it hinders you, consider other emotions that would be more functional and positive. Ask yourself what you would need to think or do to generate these emotions, and do it. Do the same with your negative attitudes or thoughts. Consider what might help you "master" the situation. If you find this exercise to be especially challenging, remember the words of Charles Popplestown: "You cannot always control circumstances, but you can control your own thoughts." During these three days, write down in your journal all your experiences and attempts to manage your emotions and attitudes.

Reflection: Answer the following questions in your journal. What was your reaction to this exercise? What were the most difficult and the easiest actions to take? What were the reactions of others when you adopted positive emotions and attitudes? What effects did expressing solely positive emotions and attitudes have on how you felt? Your level of effectiveness? Your sense of mastery? Others' reactions? What lessons have you learned about yourself and about managing your emotions and attitudes as a result of this exercise?

Action Plan: What five actions will you take starting now to (a) continue expressing positive emotions and attitudes and (b) encourage others to do the same? Keep a record of your plan and your progress in implementing your plan in your journal.

Food for thought:

- Develop a positive, constructive attitude. This will get you far in life since your attitude gives you altitude. People may be hired because they are technically competent, but they tend to get fired because of their attitudes. Think about what your attitude is saying about you right now!
- Avoid knee-jerk reactions. Breathe, calm yourself, and think about how a mature person would handle a situation.
- As Wayne Dyer said, "If you change the way you look at things, the things you look at change … How people treat you is their karma; how you react is yours." We can actively try to create the situations that we desire, and in the morning we can decide what attitude and mood we want to have that day. It's a question of recognizing when our attitudes need adjusting and our moods need managing and making it happen.
- If you're feeling bored, think about what you can do to feel energized, and do it!

10

DO YOU MAKE GREAT CHOICES?

"Think with your head, love with your heart and let your intuition make decisions." – Jim Treliving

Here's your two-part challenge: In **part 1,** think of the last decision you made, one where you had several good options or one where the solution wasn't obvious. In your journal, describe the decision and answer the following questions:

1. What process did you follow to make the decision?
2. Who did you involve in making the decision?
3. What roles did intuition or emotions play?
4. What was the end result?
5. Would you say it was a good decision? Why?
6. What would you have done differently?

Be sure to answer these questions before continuing with the rest of this exercise.

While reading the following tips, keep your answers to the questions in mind. Ask yourself which steps you skipped, if any, and whether you added steps that aren't described below. A lot has been written about the rational decision-making process. This process counts on people collecting all the information that may be pertinent to making a decision and then making an optimal decision based on objective considerations. In reality, we don't always have the time or energy to gather or analyze all the relevant information. More often than not, we do what's called satisficing – we choose a solution that is good enough based on the limited information we have. As imperfect as decision-making processes are, there are ways in which we can improve the odds of making a good decision. Here are a few steps to follow:

1. **Ask yourself, "is it important?"** Before investing your time and energy to tackle a particular problem, ask the following questions: (a) Is the problem or decision important? (b) Can the problem resolve itself? (c) Is it up to me to make a decision? (d) Will devoting time to solving the problem or making a decision make a difference? If the answer is no to any one of these questions, then you probably shouldn't be making the decision.

2. **Reflect**. Don't make decisions when you are stressed, hungry, tired, rushed, or emotional. Take the time to be in a good disposition so that you can see more clearly. What is true for you is true for others: don't expect others to make quick decisions under these circumstances. Give them time to think instead of imposing your expectations and preferences.

3. **Gather facts.** Collect as much information as you need to make a decision. But, don't fall prey to analysis paralysis – continuing to collect more and more information rather than making a decision. Identify your observations and the facts of the situation in an impersonal way. To have a clearer view of reality, distinguish between the facts and your interpretations of these facts.

4. **Consult with others.** Obtaining different perspectives can help you adopt a broader view of the situation. It's especially important to involve people who may be affected by a decision.

5. **Separate causes from symptoms.** Ask yourself "why" five times to discover the root causes of a problem. This method developed by Taiichi Ohno will give you a better idea of the origin of the problems and, therefore, possible solutions. For example, if you don't feel motivated to work, ask yourself why. The answer may be, "I don't feel like it!" So, ask yourself why again. You might say, "I don't know how to do it." By the time you ask yourself why the fifth time, you might realize that you lack confidence in your ability to do the work. This will tell you what to do to fix the problem.

6. **Use your intuition.** The previous steps asked you to dig deep into the details of the problem and its root causes. In this step, you need to take a broader view of the problem, and try to see if any patterns exist. What is the big picture? What is really happening here? What is your gut feeling telling you? Before looking for solutions, make sure that you have accurately defined the problem.

7. **Identify and evaluate several alternatives.** Identify your criteria; in other words, decide how you will evaluate the alternatives. For example, when Bob was deciding which bike to buy, one of his criteria was that he should be able to carry it to his second-floor apartment. You can also weight the criteria so that the more important ones have more influence on your choice. When identifying alternatives, be creative and do some brainstorming. It'll allow you to identify options that you may not have previously considered. Remember that maintaining the status quo – "doing nothing" – may be a valid option. By comparing several options, you'll be able to see which ones stand out from the others and seem to have the most potential in the long term.

8. **Make the decision analytically, then emotionally.** Use a logical and fact-based approach to make your decision. After finding a logical solution, consult your emotions to see how comfortable you are with your chosen solution. Does it feel right? What impact might it have on people?

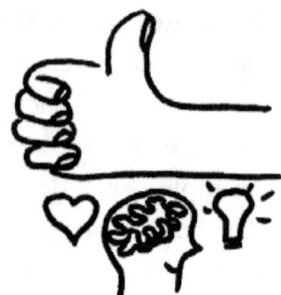

9. **Verify the quality of the decision based on six criteria**: rights, justice, compassion, role model, public opinion, and peace. Does the decision respect the rights and responsibilities of all the people involved? Is it a just or fair decision? Is the decision in line with your duty to care about others? What would your friends do if they were in the same situation as you? How would the person who, in your opinion, has the highest morality and the best judgment act in this situation? How would you feel if your family knew your decision? How would you feel if your decision was published on social networks? If you make this decision, can you get a good night's sleep? Modify your decision based on your answers to these questions.

10. **Evaluate the decision once you have made and implemented it.** Ask yourself if this was a good decision and what you would do differently the next time.

This 10 step process is especially useful when you have a complex decision to make and lots of time to gather information and reflect.

In **part 2**, we present a quick way of evaluating and making effective choices, and then we invite you to apply this process to yourself. It's based on choice theory developed by Dr. William Glasser. Choice theory has been applied in a wide range of settings including workplaces and is grounded on the idea that we are responsible for our choices, and our choices are our best attempt to get our needs met. According to Dr. Glasser, beyond basic survival needs, four needs motivate all that we do: (a) love and a sense of belonging (the most important need), (b) power (a sense of control and achievement), (c) fun (enjoyment), and (d) freedom (autonomy and independence). There is often a trade-off between power and love. If we try to exercise power over someone, we risk damaging the relationship. According to Dr. Glasser, the most important relationships and activities in our life should be meeting our needs in all four areas. So, if the diagram to the right were a pie, this means that Sue, for example, should have four good sized slices in relation to her job. Sometimes

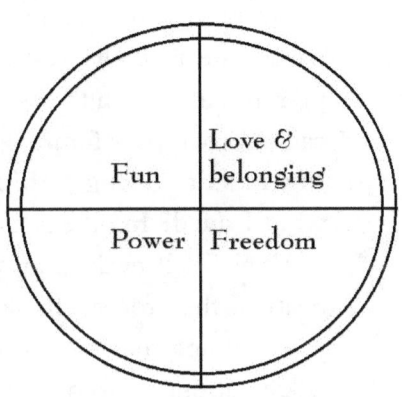

we choose effective ways of satisfying these needs, sometimes we don't. Awesome employees evaluate their choices and find a way to get their needs met in a positive, constructive fashion. More than this, however, they encourage others to do the same.

Central to choice theory is the idea that you are the only person you can control. This means that complaining, criticizing, and blaming others and victimizing yourself are ineffective behaviors. They keep you stuck in the past and don't help you move forward. Instead of bemoaning the past, Dr. Glasser suggests that we do some self-evaluation and make better choices. Here are four questions that are at the core of this process:

1. **What do I want?** The first step is to clarify what you really want. This step is more difficult than you might think. As Dr. Glasser argues, it can be easier for people to describe what they do not want rather than what they do want! For example, Coco

knows that she does not want to be in a confrontational situation, but she hasn't clarified what she wants precisely. Does she want to have friendly, harmonious relationships or just respectful interactions? Identifying what you really want is essential for making it happen.

2. **What am I doing? Thinking? Feeling?** The answers to these questions provide you with a realistic view of your current actions, thoughts, and feelings. For example, Coco may avoid conflicts, talk to Sue about her problems with Bob, or even participate in their escalation. It's important to focus on the present rather than the past. The past can't be changed, but you can improve your future if you change your behavior.

3. **Is what I'm doing / thinking / feeling helping me to get what I need?** In other words, is what you're doing working for you? This self-evaluation question is crucial. In fact, it's at the heart of the process! It allows you to become aware that what you're doing may not be working for you. You should avoid talking about symptoms, blaming, and complaints. They don't help you to get closer to what you want; rather, they just tell you what you don't want. And it's important to answer this question yourself, rather than having someone else evaluate your actions. In fact, the process works only when people who have a problem answer the question themselves. Otherwise, they may feel like they're being judged.

4. **Do I want to make a plan to get more of what I need?** Sometimes, you may not feel like making better choices. It can be easier to do what you have always done even though it would be more need-fulfilling to make some changes. Or, we may think someone else should make the first move. People tend to become comfortable with their habits, however ineffective they are. But, you can change what you choose to do, and, over time, develop new habits. It takes practice for new habits to feel natural. You can do something to get closer to

what you need, even if these are only very small steps. Focus on what you can change directly – your actions and your thoughts. Set small goals and gradually you will get closer to what you want. Develop plans that are simple, precise, and realistic. Going slowly in a positive direction is better than creating ambitious plans that are overwhelming. If your plans don't work, revisit them and simplify them even further. Be patient and supportive with yourself and others.

Part 2 of the exercise gives you practice in asking yourself these four questions. Throughout the entire week, whenever you feel that you have a choice to make or a thought/feeling/behavior to change, ask yourself the four questions just presented. For example, Bob wanted to learn as much as possible during the management seminar, but he didn't prepare for it, he spent time on his cellphone or joking around, and he took an extra-long coffee break. When he asked himself if what he was doing was helping him to achieve his goal, he realized that he was sabotaging himself. He decided to take more responsibility for his learning by preparing, participating, and being fully present. Keep track of your results in your journal.

Reflection: Answer the following questions in your journal. In part 1, were you able to see any differences between your decision-making process and the 10-step process that was described? Which steps had you left out? What additional steps, if any, did you follow to reach your decision? Regarding part 2, how challenging was this exercise? In which situations did you ask yourself the four questions? How did this questioning influence the choices you made? What did you learn about yourself in this exercise?

Action Plan: What five actions will you take starting now to (a) improve your decision-making process and (b) make choices that help you meet your needs in a positive manner? Keep a record of your plan and your progress in implementing your plan in your journal.

Food for thought:

- Get more of what you want in life by considering whether what you're doing, thinking, and feeling are standing in your way. Be prepared to take small steps toward reaching your goals.
- Be reflective about how you make decisions. Make integrity, honesty, generosity, patience, and justice your calling cards.
- "The best way to not feel hopeless is to get up and do something. Don't wait for good things to happen to you. If you go out and make some good things happen, you will fill the world with hope, you will fill yourself with hope." – Barack Obama
- "People are responsible for their own behavior. Human beings – not society, not heredity, not history – determine their own choices. People can change and live more effective lives. People need not remain victims of external forces, neither do they need to wait for the rest of the world to change before being able to satisfy their own needs." – William Glasser
- "Parties who want milk should not seat themselves on a stool in the middle of the field in the hope that the cow will back up to them." – Elbert Hubbard

11

HOW WELL DO YOU MANAGE YOUR EMAIL?

"No one ever got rich checking their email more often."
– Noah Kagan

"Turn off your email; turn off your phone; disconnect from the Internet. Figure out a way to set limits so you can concentrate when you need to, and disengage when you need to. Technology is a good servant but a bad master." – Gretchen Rubin

"Could you spend a week or even a day without reading your emails, using social media or going online?
Someone recently joked with me that having Internet access is more important than having food or water." – Nigel Cumberland

Are emails taking over your day? Your weekends? Your life? Are you constantly checking and responding to emails? Email is a convenient tool that, by and large, we use without concern for when or how it is best used. **You can easily waste an entire day responding to emails if you're not careful.** It can be tempting to respond to emails as soon as they arrive, regardless of their importance.

For example, Sue used to check and respond to emails immediately – as soon as she heard the "bing" alert that she had received an email. Then, this person would write back, and then she would, etc. In part, responding quickly to  emails set up the expectation that she was always available to whoever was writing to her, especially if she responded during the evening or weekend. Her evenings and weekends could easily be taken up with non-urgent work emails. Moreover, at work, that "bing" interrupted her concentration. And, she wouldn't get much work done when she was constantly checking her inbox. Continuing to check her emails distracted her from her work, and, at the end of the day, she wondered where the day had gone. Bottom line: **manage your emails before they manage you!**

Here are a few practices that might help you use email in service of your priorities:

1. **Stay focused on your priorities.** Do you start your day by reading and responding to emails? If so, you're giving priority to someone else's agenda, rather than focusing your energy on what is most important to you. A good habit is to **start your day by first looking at your agenda and your list of things to accomplish for the day. Those are your priorities.** Ensure that you have reserved blocks of time to work on your priorities. Sometimes, people only put appointments or deadlines on their agendas, but it's important to designate blocks of time for your priorities. Psychologically, this reminds you of your priorities, and it doesn't allow you to fritter away or assign bits and pieces of time to other things that take you away from your priorities.

It allows you to realize, for example, if someone asks you if you're available in the afternoon, that your afternoon is "booked" – you'll be engaged in your priority work.

2. **Consult emails in blocks of time.** When and how should you handle your emails? Figure out a system that works for you. Ideally, you would set aside several blocks of time throughout the day so that you could read and process your emails in batches. For example, Sue consults her emails only four times a day, 30 minutes or less each time. She does this an hour or so after she has started working, and then in two hour increments. Except for these "email periods," she keeps her email program closed so that she's not tempted to check her emails more often. To remove distractions, Sue has also removed any bells or notifications that indicate that she has received an email. During her email periods, she sends emails, she **immediately responds to those emails that require 5 minutes or less to handle**, and she notes on her list of things to do any important tasks arising from the emails that will take more time. She determines their priority level and fits them into her agenda. This allows Sue to increase her focus, productivity, and feelings of accomplishment.

3. **Keep an empty (or nearly empty) inbox.** How full is your inbox? At one point, Sue had hundreds of emails in her inbox. It was overwhelming and chaotic, and she couldn't shake the feeling that work was piling up. When Sue decide to "clear the deck" and move all these emails to an archive subfolder, it gave her an immense feeling of relief. It felt like a load had been lifted from her shoulders. Now, when a new email arrives, she acts on it (responds, adds it to a to-do list, or reads it) and then either deletes or files it.

4. **Use email only for routine messages.** You should use email when the message you want to communicate is routine and simple. When your message is non-routine, ambiguous and

complex, or when it requires immediate feedback and discussion, you should meet face to face.

5. **Answer within a reasonable period of time.** In this era of fast communication, some people may expect you to respond instantaneously to their emails. They may even (impolitely) send a follow-up email within an hour of having sent their original email, inquiring if you received it (since they didn't receive a response). However, you are the master of your email, and you can dictate your response speed. Although expectations vary, responding to an email within 24 hours (except for weekends and evenings) is usually considered to be reasonable.

6. **Remember that loose lips sink ships.** Don't use email to discuss something you wouldn't want to see on a public bulletin board or on social networks, or anything that might taint your image or that of your employer. Remember that: (a) accidents happen; (b) emails have legs; (d) emails are stored somewhere, even if you delete them; (d) emails can be monitored; and (e) emails can be used in legal proceedings. Imagine the harm and embarrassment if your inappropriate emails are shared.

7. **Be polite.** Be aware of how you compose your message. If your email is extremely brief or direct, it may come across as "giving orders" to someone, which may be offensive. A good indicator of the tone you should adopt is how you would communicate this message if you were talking to the person face to face. Be mindful of how your email might be interpreted by the recipient. A brief message can easily be misinterpreted as abrupt and impolite. An overly casual message may appear to be unprofessional. In turn, give others the benefit of the doubt when interpreting the tone of their emails. Your interpretation doesn't necessarily reflect their intentions. Be sure to check your understanding of what they have written.

8. **Think twice before sending an email (and re-read it!)**. Ask yourself: (a) "Is this the best way to deal with this issue or topic?" (b) Is the subject line informative? (c) Are there any grammatical errors? (d) Does my email have a polite and positive tone? (e) Am I sending confidential information that should not be sent via email? (f) Is my message hostile or insulting? (g) Have I overused emoticons ☺ and electronic jargon (LOL)? (h) Have I used UPPERCASE, thus giving the impression that I'm SCREAMING?

Here's your challenge: Throughout the week, adopt the following practices and see if they help you:

1. Don't let emails dictate how you organize your day. Start with your own priorities and block off specific times to check your emails; for example, once every two hours. Outside of these blocks of time, resist the urge to check your emails. Log out of your email program as soon as the block of time is complete.

2. Follow the five-minute rule when checking your emails: if you can reply to an email within five minutes, do it! Otherwise, schedule a time to respond to it in your agenda.

3. Be brief but polite. (a) Get to the point quickly and nicely. Long emails place demands on other people's time. (b) Avoid aggressiveness or bossiness in your emails. If you order someone to do something, your email won't be well received. Remember: you catch more flies with honey than with vinegar!

4. Re-read your emails and check for errors, clarity, and tone. One missed word can change the meaning of what you're trying to say. Be nice!

5. Don't send an email when you are angry. You might regret it! Sleep on it overnight if possible. And don't write in an email what you wouldn't want to see on the front page of the newspaper.

Keep track of your results in your journal.

Reflection: Answer the following questions in your journal. How challenging was this exercise? What were the most difficult and easy actions to take? Which tips helped you to regain control of your inbox? What were the benefits of scheduling blocks of email time? Are there any other practices that you adopted that help you use email effectively? What lessons have you learned in doing this exercise?

Action Plan: What five actions will you take starting now to manage your emails more effectively? Keep a record of your plan and your progress in implementing your plan in your journal.

12

ARE YOU A TIME WASTER OR A TIME INVESTOR?

"Most of us say yes to too much stuff, and then we let these little, mediocre things fill our lives." – Derek Sivers

"I try to take one day at a time, but sometimes several days attack me at once. I could do great things, if I weren't so busy doing little things." – Ashley Brilliant

"The wisdom of life consists in the elimination of non-essentials." – Lin Yutang

"Tomorrow will be the same as today unless you do something about it now. Can you afford not to?" – Unknown

You may have heard it before: everyone has the same 168 hours in a week. There are 60 minutes an hour no matter what we do. All of us have all the time there is. There is nothing we can do to manage time. How we use our time is the only thing that we really have control over. Not having enough time is not the problem; being able to manage within the time that we have available is the challenge. At every moment, either consciously or unconsciously, we are making choices about how to invest that time. Or waste it.

When we waste our time, we feel like a hamster on a wheel. Day-to-day life becomes an endless cycle of activities that don't seem to get us anywhere. Some people get a great deal done while others struggle with a lighter workload. There are six key things 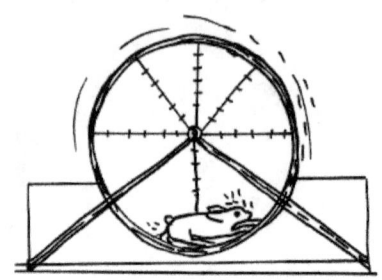 that tend to stop us from investing our time well and stepping off the hamster wheel:

1. **We don't realize that we're running on the hamster wheel.** Our habits feel comfortable, and we're simply not aware that there are alternatives. Days, weeks, months pass by and nothing much has changed. We're busy, but we're not advancing in life. In his book *Tools of Titans*, Tim Ferriss doesn't mince words about what it means to be busy. He says that "Busy = out of control. Lack of time is lack of priorities. If I'm 'busy,' it is because I've made choices that put me in that position ... If I'm too busy, it's a cue to re-examine my systems and rules. Being busy is a form of laziness – lazy thinking and indiscriminate action. Being busy is more often used as an excuse for avoiding the few critically important but uncomfortable actions."

2. **We lack focus and are easily distracted.** We're driven to distraction, and our attention is being diverted from more important stuff. It is easy to rationalize filling our time with television, Internet searches, social media, video games, texting, and other sources of entertainment and instant gratification. Distractions numb our awareness that we are on the wheel. When we're having trouble resisting temptation in the moment

and keeping the big picture in mind, we should ask ourselves, "What is the absolute best use of my time right now?" Usually, the best use of your time is to do one thing at a time and stay with it until it's done. In trying to multitask, we spread our attention too thin, we lose focus, and nothing gets done well or we leave a bunch of projects started but unfinished. Concentrating on one thing at a time allows us to use our time more efficiently. According to Piers Steel, an expert on procrastination at the University of Calgary, a great way to deal with temptations directly is to make them inaccessible or difficult to use (for example, unplugging or selling the television, or not having the Internet at home). Also, you can get some of your needs met before they become an overwhelming siren call; for example, taking 10 minutes to have some fun before you start working. Finally, he suggests that you create disincentives that will make your temptations unappealing; for example, agreeing to pay a friend a certain amount of money if you can't meet a particular deadline.

3. **We think that running on the hamster wheel is a good thing; after all, "everyone's doing it."** We tend to confuse activities with results. Being busy does not necessarily mean that we are accomplishing what we should be accomplishing. There is a difference between being efficient and being effective. Efficiency means doing things right, effectiveness means doing the right things right. Many of us spend lots of time carrying out activities for which we have done very little planning. Yet one principle of time management is that, on average, every hour invested in planning an activity saves approximately three to four hours in carrying out that activity. So, for every minute that you spend planning or thinking about what you will do, you will save approximately three to four minutes in executing your plan, usually with better results. Another time management principle is Pareto's 80/20 law. Pareto was a nineteenth century

Italian economist who noted that 80% of the wealth in his country was held by 20% of the people. He also noted that, in almost any human endeavor, 80% of the effective results come about through 20% of the efforts, and, conversely, approximately 80% of the efforts produce 20% of the results. Those who are able to identify and plan to carry out activities in their 20% effectiveness are usually the best managers of time. The idea in effective time management is to "work smarter not harder."

4. **Our biggest priorities may seem overwhelming** to us, too overwhelming to start right now. We say we'll get around to it, but we just put it off and don't get started. The routine of running on the wheel can seem easier than the giant step involved in pursuing our biggest priorities. Big priorities are best approached one bite at a time. If you're having trouble getting started on a major task, slice it into small, manageable tasks, each of which could be done in a limited amount of time. This helps you build momentum.

5. **We wait until we feel motivated** to begin a project without realizing that motivation is something that usually happens after we have started the project. We're waiting for the perfect time, circumstances, and inspiration to step off the wheel, not realizing that this doesn't exist. This indecision or lack of action is a decision not to decide; i.e., procrastination. Many people spend more time putting things off and feeling anxious about doing so than they actually spend working on them. To counter procrastination, use the balance sheet method. On the left side of a sheet of paper, make a list of all the reasons you're procrastinating on a particular project. On the right side, list all the benefits of going ahead and getting the job done. The effect is striking. On the left side, you will usually have only one or two excuses, such as "it might involve an awkward conversation" or "I'm waiting for the perfect conditions." On

the right side, you may find a long list of benefits, including the feeling of relief that comes with getting a necessary but sometimes unpleasant task behind you.

6. **We simply don't get started.** As Jeremey Statton says in his blog, the secret formula for accomplishing goals is to: "(a) Start; (b) Take a first step; (c) Take the next step after that; (d) Repeat; (e) Overcome obstacles; (f) Finish." Like Jeremy says, this isn't really a secret formula – everyone knows that to finish a project, you need to start the project and keep working on it. It takes time and effort that we might rather use for something more immediately rewarding, and it can be hard to see the benefits of what we're doing in the short term. But it's the only path to success. We want the outcome or results, but all the work that is required can be daunting. The only way to achieve the goal is to persist and make a habit out of what we're trying to do. But, more often than not, we simply avoid taking that first step off the wheel in the direction of our priorities. Inertia keeps us trapped.

Can you relate to any of these causes of time wasting? The solutions offered in the discussion above can help you move toward time investing. But what else do time investors do that set them apart from time wasters? If you're a time investor, you:

1. **Have a sense of purpose and direction that provides focus to your efforts.** You have set goals for yourself that are meaningful. It might be helpful to use the 100th birthday technique to develop long-term objectives. Imagine that a reporter is interviewing you on your 100th birthday. The reporter asks you to name the things that you're most proud of. Visualize the end result as if it had already happened and answer this question as specifically as possible. Based on your 100th birthday goals, identify intermediate goals (for example, targets for 5 or 10 years from now) and short-term goals for the next

six months or year. Develop action steps and deadlines for undertaking them.

2. **Identify your top priorities each day.** This is what must get done for you to feel happy with your day. Don't put second things first. Learn to discriminate between what must be done, what could be done, and what you would like to do. Determine when you do your best work, and schedule your priorities during these blocks of time. Tim Ferriss says that we should take the three things that we least want to do and have been putting off for whatever reason and ask ourselves, "If these were the only things I accomplished today, would I be satisfied with my day?" If the answer is yes, then he suggests that we block off a period of three hours or so on our calendar to get them done and out of the way.

3. **Make your agenda your friend.** The busiest people are able to find time for what they want to do, not because they have any more time than others but because they think in terms of "making" time through careful scheduling. They don't only schedule events – meetings, appointments, and deadlines – they also schedule thinking time, a block of time for important tasks, and an hour a day of uncommitted time. Just like Tim Ferriss suggests, they spend at least one substantial block of time each day working on an important task. And they do this as early in the day as possible, so they don't feel panicky as the day goes on.

4. **Avoid distractions.** Time investors focus on top priorities rather than busy work, distractions, or anything that might keep them from their top priorities. They don't feel the need to respond immediately to emails and other demands on their time.

5. **Keep the top of your desk clean.** They keep on their desks only the project they're working on. They organize their desks so that paper shuffling is minimized, and the material they need

to access is within reach. They avoid the "Stacked Desk Syndrome" where the stacked items become a constant source of mental interruption and anxiety.

6. **Analyze how you're investing your time** and continually improve your use of time.

7. **Avoid reverse delegation**, which is what happens when someone tries to offload their work onto you. It's important to be able to (politely) say no to others' demands on your time when saying yes will jeopardize achieving your goals. According to Derek Sivers, "Most of us say yes to too much stuff, and then we let these little, mediocre things fill our lives."

8. **Make realistic time estimates**. Remember Murphy's laws: (a) Everything takes longer than you think (20% longer!); (b) Nothing is as simple as it seems; and (c) If anything can go wrong, it will. In setting deadlines, expect the unexpected and allow time, where possible, for your own and others' errors.

9. **Take time to relax and reward yourself for work well done.** Give yourself frequent, small rewards for accomplishing difficult tasks. Even small breaks can serve as rewards.

10. **Involve others and ask for help.** Don't try to go it alone; people are often willing and able to help. They can help you set priorities, do some of the tasks, share what works for them, and support you in meeting your goals (for example, not interrupting you or offering temptations, and not being late with their part of the work).

11. **Avoid doing eight stupid things.** Including procrastination which involves actively avoiding getting something done (like not having a medical problem checked), David Perkins, a creativity and learning expert at Harvard, says that eight stupid things block our progress in life: (a) impulsiveness (acting too quickly, losing your temper, etc.), (b) neglect (ignoring something or acting too late), (c) vacillation (hesitating over a decision), (d) backsliding (adopting a new behavior such as

quitting smoking but then falling back into old behaviors), (e) indulging yourself (falling into a pattern of excess such as too much TV), (f) overdoing an activity (such as over-preparing for a presentation), and (g) and what he calls "walking the edge" (trying to avoid a certain behavior such as overcommitting yourself and finding yourself on the edge of backsliding). David Perkins says that these are all forms of under-management. We're not conscious of what we're doing in the moment. He says, "When we feel ourselves becoming irritable, we can try to step out of the situation, metaphorically or sometimes literally. When we feel an outburst in the making, we can engage in the classic strategy of counting to ten. When we discover that we're about to give up on an important task, we can try to motivate ourselves with a pep talk. Unfortunately, managing the moment is not easy. People may be too absorbed in the situation itself. They only recognize later that they might have tried to take themselves in hand, or they recognize this fleetingly but cannot summon enough focus to try."

Which of these time investing tips in both lists are you prepared to try? Select at least three of them to use when you're doing this week's challenge.

Here's your challenge: Your challenge is to prepare an inventory of your time use over a period of three "typical" days in your journal. This inventory will help you develop a clearer picture of how you're actually using your time, your biggest time wasters, and what you can do to get rid of them. At the beginning of each day, take a few minutes to write down your three biggest priorities for the day and to review your preferred time investing tips. Then, from waking up to bedtime, write down everything you do in 15-minute intervals in your journal. Here is an example:

Time	Activity
7 – 7:15	Breakfast
7:15 – 7:30	Getting dressed and ready to go to work
...	...

Once you have prepared your inventory for the three-day period:

1. Review your inventory and create a list of categories that describe how you used your time (for example, checking email, preparing and eating meals, Internet searches, watching movies, writing reports, etc.).

2. For each of these categories, indicate the number of 15-minute time blocks you spent engaged in that activity over the three days, and then calculate your average for a day (for example: Checking email = 21 time blocks over 3 days = an average of 7 time blocks or 105 minutes per day).

3. Then, draw a pie chart that represents how you used your time on average during one day. For example, you're awake from 7 am to 11 pm on average, which consists of 16 hours or 960 minutes. Checking email for 105 minutes represents about 11% (105/960 minutes) of your day, so you would draw a slice that covers about 11% of the pie. You can use Excel to help you do this, or you can do it manually.

Reflection: Answer the following questions in your journal. What does your pie chart reveal about your use of your time? How do you spend most of your time? What does your inventory reveal about your priorities? Was most of your time spent on what is most important to you? Which activities yielded the greatest benefits for you (in terms of productivity, feelings of energy or relaxation, etc.)? Which activities were the least helpful in this regard? What did you do to try to balance your use of time between work and leisure? How do you typically keep track of and develop an understanding of how you use your time? How often do you do this? To what extent do you plan your work (setting clear objectives and timetables) and then work your plan? To what extent did you allow others to infringe on, influence, dictate, or control how you use your time? To what extent did you consciously try to reduce wasting your time and increase investing in your time?

Action Plan: What three specific actions will you take starting now to (a) avoid time wasting, (b) increase time investing, and (c) encourage others to make the best use of their time? Keep a record of your plan and your progress in implementing your plan in your journal.

Food for thought:

- How you manage your time is your choice. You can choose to waste it and let it slip through your fingers or invest it in the important things in your life.
- Each of us has many opportunities to say "yes" to many activities, diversions, and priorities. There's usually no shortage of things to do. But there's only one you. Being willing to say "no" and focus on what is most important to you will give you the time and space you need to create a happy and productive life.

PART 3:
BUILDING
RELATIONSHIPS

13

ARE YOU A CIVIL PERSON?

"Civility costs nothing, and buys everything."
– Mary Wortley Montagu

"To put it very simply, people are rude when they are: (1) stressed;
(2) unhappy; (3) rushed. There are more and more people in this
country to whom all three happen at the same time.
Rudeness is a symptom of a bad state of mind."
– ReadyinTX (quoted by P.M. Forni)

"If you want to make friends, go out of your way to do things for
other people – things that require time, energy, unselfishness, and
thoughtfulness … A kind word or a kind act is like lighting
another man's candle with your own, which loses none of its
brightness by what the other gains." – Lawrence Lovasik

Most people would say that they are civil people. And it's easy to be
civil when everything is going our way. But what happens when you
are tired or stressed or when you're not getting what you want from
others? Are you short tempered? Do you tend to focus on your
wants and needs at the expense of those of others? Do you blow

up? Thomas Merton once said that no man is an island, and this is no truer than in today's social world. Everything we do has an impact on others. To focus solely on what we want is to ignore our responsibilities to others and the impact that we're having on them.

If you want to be an awesome employee, you must be civil. Civility involves showing respect for others. In part, this means showing respect for others' time by being reliable and predictable – being on time for meetings, returning phone calls and emails rapidly, meeting deadlines, following through on commitments, not having to excuse oneself for lateness, and not requiring that people wait for you while you finish getting ready. Some people excuse themselves for being late because they're "busy." But people who use this excuse are no busier than others; they simply don't manage their use of time well nor are they respectful of others' time. This is essentially saying that others are less important than them. Respectful folks plan for unforeseen impediments; they try not to overload their agenda or underestimate how much time it takes to get to a meeting. Being unreliable is one of many ways of being uncivil. Here are a few others:

- Using your cellphone while interacting with someone or while in a meeting or social gathering.
- Not cleaning up after yourself wherever you are.
- Doing private things in public (grooming, etc.).
- Excluding others or not showing interest in what they have to say.
- Not taking responsibility for yourself; frequently making excuses or asking for exceptions.
- Taking credit for others' work.
- Not helping when needed.
- Being unprepared or inattentive or not participating during meetings.
- Imposing your perspective on others.

- Humiliating others, making jokes at their expense, or insulting them.
- Shouting at someone, pouting or screaming when you don't get your way.
- Complaining, blaming, and being negative.
- Focusing exclusively on what you want.

Can you think of other examples? There are lots of them!

Incivility erodes trust. It's hard to trust someone who seems excessively focused on themselves at the expense of others. In his *Scientific American* article on the neurobiology of trust, Paul Zak argues that we are wired to trust, but negative experiences hamper that ability. When people are unpredictable or asocial, this uncertainty and isolation makes us less trusting. According to Paul Zak, we can earn others' trust through "diligence, fidelity and applied effort." To do so, he offers several suggestions:

- Keep your promises; follow through on your commitments.
- Realize that your actions are either contributing to or eroding your "brand" (your reputation).
- Be truthful in your communications with others.
- Be willing to help others and make it easy to interact with you.
- Manage your moods so people know what to expect from you.
- Help people feel safe around you by being empathetic and encouraging.

- Share information that will help others.
- Celebrate others' accomplishments.
- Be polite. Ask, don't order. Say please, thank you, you're welcomed, and I'm sorry.

Here's your two-part challenge: In **part 1**, to help you determine how civil you are in your day-to-day life (work, home, school, and other commitments), over the next week, take an inventory of your behaviors when interacting with others. Describe in your journal the occasions when you were uncivil and examples of when you were civil. Also, take note of others' uncivil and civil behaviors. In **part 2**, try to be incredibly civil in all of your interactions with other during the week.

Reflection: Answer the following questions in your journal. How challenging was this exercise for you? What examples of uncivil and civil behaviors did you identify? What was the context of these behaviors? Were you (or the other person) feeling rushed? Responding to others' incivility? In relation to the uncivil behaviors, how did you tend to "excuse" your behavior (if at all)? What impression do you think this behavior left with others? To what extent do you think you came across as a leader? When you noticed others being uncivil (late, unreliable, etc.), what was your impression of them? How challenging was it to be incredibly civil? How did others react? What lessons have you learned in doing this exercise?

Action Plan: What specific actions will you take starting now to: (a) ensure that you are behaving civilly; (b) eliminate uncivil behaviors from your repertoire; and (c) encourage others to be civil? Keep a record of your plan and your progress in implementing your plan in your journal.

14

ARE YOU A ZINGER SLINGER?

"Remember … whoever is trying to bring you down is already below you." – Ziad K. Abdelnour

"A sarcastic person has a superiority complex that can be cured only by the honesty of humility …Get into the habit of putting a kind interpretation on all you see and hear, and of having kind thoughts of everyone of whom you think. Never say behind a man's back what you are ashamed to say to his face."
– Lawrence Lovasik

According to *Merriam-Webster*, a zinger is "a quick and clever comment that criticizes or insults someone." Zingers are subtle, causticm ambiguous, veiled disparaging pokes whose nasty intentions are deniable ("I was just kidding; don't take it so seriously!"). David Eddie calls these denials "cloaking devices" and offers two terrific examples: "the 'insultiment' (insult + compliment = insultiment): 'Oooh, those glasses look good on you, they really distract from all the weight you've gained recently.' Or the 'questionsult' (question + insult = questionsult): 'Oooh, so you finally got new curtains? Were these your first choice?'"

126

Here are some more examples:

- Your hair's so curly. Did you put your finger in a socket? (Sarcasm, mockery, put-downs)
- I wish I were as confident as you to wear something so tight-fitting! (Innuendos)
- You always/You never ___ (Exaggerating; blaming; suggesting that there's a pattern)
- Yes, but ... (Discounting; seeming to agree, but not really)
- I'm sorry but ... (Seeming to apologize, but not really)
- I was too busy ... (Persistent excuses)
- You're just too smart for me (Belittling)
- Eye rolling (Contempt; passive-aggressiveness)

It goes without saying that awesome employees don't use zingers. Using zingers signals a lack of respect for another person. They destroy rather than build relationships with others. Indeed, Tom Laforce calls them the opposite of assertiveness: instead of  being respectful, honest, and direct, zingers are disrespectful, not entirely honest, and indirect. They're an indirect way of communicating your message.

If you're on the receiving end of zingers, don't buy into what the person is saying, don't get defensive, and don't respond with zingers in a tit for tat manner. These may be precisely the responses that are sought; but, more than that, they will not contribute to having a constructive conversation. One possible response is to ask the person to repeat himself. They are usually reluctant to do so because they may be embarrassed by their own statement. Tom Laforce offers another interesting option: "The next time someone pulls one of these on you, ask, 'What are you trying to say?' The person will likely deny any hidden message. This is when you come back with, 'No, I think you want to tell me something. I'm just not sure I understand what it is. Please be clearer.' With those two comments you've told people doing this that you've caught them (they hate that), and you've invited them to communicate more assertively. Respond in this manner consistently and chances are some of the people who most often use passive-aggressive behaviors will go find another target, and maybe even change their methods."

Here's your challenge: To help you become aware of zingers in your repertoire and that of others and to help you extinguish them from your vocabulary, we invite you to pay special attention to whether you or other people use zingers over the next week. Also, use the options indicated in the previous paragraph for responding to zingers. Do not laugh at zingers that you overhear others directing at other people. This only encourages them to continue slinging zingers. Also, if you find yourself directing a zinger at someone, apologize immediately in front of everyone who heard it. Record your findings and efforts in your journal.

Reflection: Answer the following questions in your journal. How frequently did you hear others using zingers during the three-day period? What did they say? In what context? How did you feel? How did you respond? What was their reaction? How about yourself: what zingers did you find yourself using? What was the reaction of the person you targeted and others who may have heard your zinger? How did you handle this situation? What lessons did you learn about using zingers in conversations?

Action plan: What five actions will you take starting now to (a) stop slinging zingers and (b) encourage others to do the same? Keep a record of your plan and your progress in implementing your plan in your journal.

15

ARE YOU A GOOD COMMUNICATOR?

"One often hears the remark: 'He talks too much', but has anyone ever heard the criticism: 'He listens too much'?"
– Norman Augustine

"We have two ears and one mouth so that we can listen twice as much as we speak." – Epictetus

"It is the province of knowledge to speak and it is the privilege of wisdom to listen." – Oliver Wendell Holmes

"Between what I think, what I want to say, what I believe I say, what I say, what you want to hear, what you believe you hear, what you hear, what you think you understand, what you want to understand, and what you understand, there are ten possibilities for difficulties in communicating." – Bernard Werber

Are you a good communicator? Do you take the time to listen? Are you better in groups or interacting one-on-one with someone? Can you adapt to the needs of different people? Have you asked for feedback about your communication skills?

Good communication starts with effective listening. As simple as listening can seem, it's really quite challenging. To really listen to another person we have to temporarily put our thoughts on hold and focus on that person and what they're saying. Sometimes we interrupt others because we want to show interest in what they're saying or because we have questions for them. Our intentions may be good but the effect is to cut off the other person. The best way to show interest is simply to listen; often the person talking to us will answer all the questions we have if we simply let them say what they have to say. We may think we're listening because we're looking in their direction, but what's going on in our minds while they're speaking? For example, are we thinking about what we're going to say, getting ready to challenge what they're saying, thinking about our own experiences, or being distracted by other factors – this person's accent, what they're wearing, or noise in the environment? These are all signs that we're not really listening.

According to Valérie Lanctôt-Bédard, coach and specialist in nonviolent communication, there are several additional signs that we haven't been listening to what the person has been expressing: responding by giving unsolicited advice (this comes across as a criticism), consoling ("oh poor you"), redirecting the conversation to ourselves ("I had a long day too"), and belittling what the person is saying ("it's not so bad"). All of these have the effect of stopping the conversation.

Valérie Lanctôt-Bédard considers listening to be a gift that we offer to others. We must therefore make sure that we are available to listen and to focus on others instead of bringing everything back to ourselves. Easy, you say? Of course, this may seem normal or natural, but actually doing it requires a lot of self-control and generosity.

To listen better, avoid:

- Interrupting and trying to respond quickly.
- Texting or doing something else on your cellphone while someone is talking with you.
- Attaching more importance to facts than to emotions when a person speaks. You need to listen to the entire message: the facts, the emotions, their nonverbal cues, and the essence of what the person is trying to get across.
- Reacting to words that you consider to be taboo.
- Quickly refuting or discounting a person's statement if you don't fully understand what they are saying or if you disagree with any part of it.
- Pretending to listen by, for example, looking in their direction but thinking about something else.
- Abandoning or ending the conversation when you consider it a difficult subject.
- Being easily distracted by elements outside the conversation (other people, TV, your cellphone).
- Criticizing the accent, appearance, or clothing of this person.
- Trying to judge or evaluate this person.

- Thinking more about what you're going to say than what this person is saying.
- Answering even before a question is fully asked.
- Making assumptions about the other person's intentions or expectations.

Instead, you should try to:
- Share responsibility for communication. Don't give one-word responses, but don't give a speech either.
- Focus on what the person is saying. Put away distractions such as your cellphone.
- Listen to the full meaning of the message; that is, the feelings of the other person beyond the information transmitted.
- Look for important themes. What is this person really trying to tell you?
- Look at the person and lean toward them (rather than away from them).
- Observe the person's non-verbal signs.
- Adopt an attitude of openness toward your conversation partner. Leave all judgment aside.
- Show interest in what the other person is saying. Let the person know that you're listening by saying "yes", "hmm …" and leaving moments of silence in the conversation.
- Try to understand first and then be understood. Ask questions of clarification, paraphrase and reflect the feelings of the person, and check for understanding. Say, "If I understand correctly …" when someone tells you something that is more than a few sentences. Finish your paraphrasing with "is that right?" or "did I understand correctly?"
- Ask open-ended questions that require more than yes or no as an answer.

- Demonstrate understanding and empathy. Rob Goffee and Gareth Jones suggest "tough empathy": focusing on what is needed in a situation rather then what people say they want.
- Listen to what you're feeling as you listen.
- Avoid getting defensive when you hear something you don't agree with (for example, criticism).
- Make eye contact, stop what you're doing, and look at the other person.
- Allow moments of silence.
- If you're not available for a conversation, excuse yourself.

When expressing yourself, avoid:
- Starting a conversation when the other person is obviously busy with something else.
- Dominating the conversation. Share it, don't take over!
- Rapidly discounting what the person is saying without asking further questions or trying to understand their point of view.
- Being cold, passive, and disengaged. Not contributing to the conversation.
- Changing the topic to something that interests you more.
- Offering unasked-for advice as though the other person would be helpless without it.
- Focusing on yourself, your wants, your needs, your experience, your … you!
- One-upmanship: whatever news the other person has, yours is better (or worse).
- Trying to defend yourself, justify, or counter-attack.
- Complaining; assigning negative meaning to all things in life.
- Interpreting everything a person has to say as a personal attack.
- Always taking the opposite perspective of what the person is saying.

- Ignoring and not listening to what the person is saying; continuing to talk or walk away.
- Criticizing the person in front of others.
- Making negative assumptions about the person and their intentions.
- Projecting your own fears and biases onto the person.
- Complaining, blaming, criticizing, and generally being negative.
- Spreading, sharing, or listening to rumors about others.
- Making general statements without backing them up with specific facts.
- Using vocabulary and words that people don't like to hear.
- Using generalities instead of precise and concrete statements.
- Introducing topics that are off topic.
- Presenting your arguments in terms of all or nothing. Not being willing to see the other side or compromise.

Instead, here are some behaviors to adopt:
- Stay on the topic at hand.
- Use the words of the other person to build rapport.
- Use the other person's name.
- Be brief and clear in saying what you have to say.
- Adopt a friendly, warm, and respectful tone. Smile!
- Excuse yourself if you have said something inappropriate.
- Point out the positive things about the other person. Show appreciation. Thank the person.
- Ensure that your verbal and non-verbal language is consistent. For example, don't say that you're open to what the other person has to say and then cross your arms.
- Think before you speak. As Abraham Lincoln once said, "It is better to remain silent and be thought a fool, than to open your mouth and remove all doubt."

- Say what you need or feel without blaming others.
- Be willing to share your thoughts and feelings. Transparent, authentic people hide very little in their relationships with others. Their intentions and opinions are clear to all. As a result, others are less likely to misinterpret what they say and do.
- Share your successes with others in a humble manner; don't brag.
- Stay calm. Deal with negative feelings in a constructive manner.
- Know what your intentions are and what you want to achieve through communication.
- Show flexibility and openness to changing your opinion and receiving feedback.
- Rapidly move to resolve any misunderstandings.
- Stay aware and sensitive to what is happening between you and others.
- Appear enthusiastic (not monotone or bored with what you're saying).
- Use "we," "us" and "our" if you're trying to create a sense of commonality and harmony with the other person.
- Be honest, but diplomatic; avoid lying to others.
- Have a sense of humor about difficult situations.
- Share credit with others.
- Make what you have to say more personal, concrete and memorable through stories, examples, or experiences.

Here's your 4-part challenge: Your challenge this week is to neutralize your communication weaknesses and transform them into strengths. You'll do this by becoming aware of your weaknesses and appreciating their negative impact on your interactions with others. Then, you will plan and practice alternative behaviors.

In **part 1**, over a three-day period, pay special attention to your interactions with others. Try to practice all of the positive communication skills presented above. Although some of the techniques may seem mechanical at first, they will become natural and you will feel more connected to the person you're communicating with. Record the frequency of positive and negative communications in your journal paying particular attention to how often you engaged in the positive communication skills and the behaviors to avoid. Also, try to become aware of what you experience and others' reactions when you communicate. For any negative behaviors, reflect on their advantages and disadvantages.

In **part 2**, during this same three-day period, ask your supervisor and at least one coworker to give you some feedback on your communication skills. If they read the lists presented earlier, they'll be able to point out specific behaviors that you engage in. Ask for examples if anything is unclear. Ask them what you should continue doing, stop doing, and start doing as a way of enhancing your communication skills. Remember to thank them for their time and effort in providing you with feedback.

In **part 3**, review your observations and the feedback with your feedback team, look for patterns (recurring behaviors), and create a list of your top five strengths and your top five weaknesses. Ask for their help in preparing a plan to address your communications. Set some objectives, for example, reducing negative communication (such as interrupting, blaming, or defending yourself) and increasing positive communication (such as listening before expressing your opinion). Then, create a "stop, start, continue" contract indicating the behaviors that you will eliminate, those that you'll start, and those that you'll continue doing.

In **part 4**, over the next three days, put your contract into action. Pay attention to how challenging it is to change your established habits. Prior to especially challenging situations, try to follow Peter Drucker's advice. This management guru suggests that feedback analysis helps people move to more constructive behaviors. It involves writing down the anticipated results of your behaviors before you attempt them and then, after you've taken action, compare your anticipated results with what actually happened. Over time, your ability to anticipate what will likely happen in a situation will improve.

Keep track of your efforts in your journal.

Reflection: Answer the following questions in your journal. How did you feel when you were practicing your listening and expressing skills? How did the other person react? Do you think you understood more deeply what the person was trying to communicate? Were you better able to communicate your ideas? Which tips were especially challenging to follow? Why? What lessons did you learn about listening and expressing yourself?

Action Plan: What five specific actions will you take starting today to: (a) improve your listening skills; (b) improve your expressing skills, and (c) help others build their communication skills? Write them down in your journal. Keep a record of your plan and your progress in implementing your plan in your journal.

Food for thought:

- Build constructive relationships with others. Show an interest in other people as individuals. To have an amazing conversation, find out what they're passionate about!
- "You have not lived today until you have done something for someone who can never repay you." – John Bunyan

16

ARE THE FOUR HORSEMEN KILING YOUR INTERACTIONS?

"An eye for an eye will only make the whole world blind."
– Mahatma Gandhi

"Kind words can be short and easy to speak,
but their echoes are truly endless." – Mother Teresa

In his research with couples, psychologist John Gottman and his team found that, after observing couples interact with each other for only a matter of seconds, they can predict with 93% accuracy whether the couples were headed for divorce.

In particular, they found that there were four horsemen, or predictors, of divorce: **criticism, defensiveness, contempt, and stonewalling**.

Criticism consists of excessive, non-constructive negative judgements about a person (for example: "You're so lazy!") that are experienced as an attack on that person. This is especially true when people talk in absolute terms such as "You always ..." or "You never ..." When people are defensive, they place themselves in the role of a victim, and they aren't considering how they may share responsibility for the problem. They might make excuses or blame the other person for problems. When people express contempt, the most serious of the horsemen, they consider themselves to be above others. They express disrespect and condescension toward the other person. They may roll their eyes, sneer, mock, or put down others to make them feel small (for example: "You look like hell."). Finally, stonewalling, which often happens when a person is overwhelmed with the conversation and needs to distance himself, involves the silent treatment, changing the subject, or withdrawing from the conversation, perhaps even by leaving the room.

You can see how these four horsemen would be toxic to any type of relationship including workplace relationships. When interactions are dominated by accusations, negativity, a lack of respect, derision, and avoidance behaviors, a poisonous work climate develops. This toxic behavior erodes trust and negatively affects productivity.

The first thing you should do is **notice whether or not the four horsemen are present in any of your interactions** with your supervisor, fellow team members, customers, or others. If this is the case, you should plan alternative behaviors that would contribute to a more positive atmosphere. You shouldn't just assume that everything will simply resolve itself. Usually, the opposite happens as people stew in their destructive feelings.

As an alternative to criticism, you should try to **voice your concerns – in a gentle fashion – from your own perspective using "I" statements** to refer to how you feel about a specific behavior (don't make not a global attack). Instead of responding to criticism with defensiveness ("Yes, but"), try to listen carefully to what the other person is saying, and accept responsibility and apologize for your part of the problem ("The part I agree with is…"). As Dale Carnegie once said, "Any fool can criticize, complain, and condemn – and most fools do. But it takes character and self-control to be understanding and forgiving."

Contempt should be replaced with consideration of the person's positive qualities and attributes, and describing your own needs in the relationship. Sometimes simple solutions such as expressing your appreciation for someone prove to be the most effective. As Leo Buscaglia says, "Too often we underestimate the power of a touch, a smile, a kind word, a listening ear, an honest compliment, or the smallest act of caring, all of which have the potential to turn a life around."

If you need to emotionally distance yourself in an interaction, it is perfectly acceptable to ask for a few minutes to collect your thoughts before you continue the conversation. In this manner, the other person won't think that you have abandoned or rejected them. Finally, it might be worthwhile to consider the following advice from Mary Ann Pietzker: "Before sharing your opinion about something, you should ask yourself four questions: **'Is what I'm about to say kind? It is true? Is it necessary? Does it improve upon the silence?'**" If your answer to these questions is yes, then go ahead and share your opinion. Have you ever stopped yourself from saying something potentially hurtful and been relieved that you did so?

Finally, keep in mind Stephen Covey's advice: "**People have an emotional bank account for each relationship; we make deposits when we are trusting, empathetic, and dependable.** We make withdrawals when we are inconsiderate, dishonest, and arbitrary. When our accounts become overdrawn, we have to be especially careful about everything we say in case it is misinterpreted. It leads to defensiveness in which people are most concerned about defending themselves."

Here's your challenge: To help you become aware of the presence of the four horsemen in your interactions with people, we invite you to pay attention to their presence in your interactions this week. Also, try to avoid these four horsemen. If you're guilty of criticism, defensiveness, contempt, and stonewalling, attempt to repair the situation by apologizing and moving the conversation to more positive ground. Keep a record of your observations and efforts in your journal.

Reflection: Answer the following questions in your journal. Where and how did these horsemen show up in your interactions this week? When and with whom have you experienced or dished out criticism, defensiveness, contempt, and stonewalling? What did they say or do, and how did you respond? How did this impact your relationship? How challenging was it to avoid the horsemen? How did others react? How did you feel during this exercise? What lessons have you learned in doing this exercise?

Action plan: Based on your reflection, describe what you can do to repair any damage to a relationship that has occurred as a result of these four horsemen. Develop a plan to have a "recovery" conversation with the other person. This will allow you to move from the "attack and defend" mode to conciliation and, eventually, collaboration. Describe what you will do to respond differently the next time the four horsemen ride into your interactions. Keep a record of your plan and your progress in implementing your plan in your journal.

17
....

ARE YOU PREPARED TO RESOLVE A CONFLICT?

"Those who'll play with cats must expect to be scratched."
– Miguel de Cervantes

"A way through conflict opens when you see that the cause is not the other people who seem to be opposing you – it is the way you perceive those people and the assumptions you make about them that create the problem." – Miles Sherts

Where there are people, there are differences in opinions, goals, and ways of doing things. Handled immediately, constructively, and respectfully with a dash of flexibility, these differences can strengthen relationships. But, left to fester, polarize, and build up, they  transform into conflict. As these conflicts or misunderstandings accumulate over time, they can feel like heavy burdens that weigh you down. Here are 10 tips for getting that weight off your back:

1. **Minimize the number of conflicts that need to be managed in the first place!** Be proactive in dealing with issues as they arise. Small irritants become big issues if not dealt with as they arise. Take responsibility and admit your error or your contribution to a misunderstanding when appropriate. Don't automatically assume that someone has bad intentions. Sometimes, people do things without thinking. Clarify your expectations and understandings and that of others. Exercise self-control. Don't feel that you have to react to everything that doesn't fit with your preferences. And, have a filter: don't say everything that's on your mind. Exercise some restraint. Have a sense of humor. Build relationships one step at a time. Simply being nice to others goes a long way to prevent conflict. Finally, as Naval Ravikant, CEO of AngelList, suggests, "Don't hang around people who are consistently engaging in conflict … People who regularly fight with others will eventually fight with you."

2. **Develop personal awareness of what you contribute to conflict or misunderstandings.** For example, do you always try to get your way, believing that you are right and the other person is wrong? Do you think that you deserve special treatment, and that the rules don't apply to you? Are you a perpetual bully or victim? Do you jump to conclusions? Are things/people/situations rarely "right" for you? Do you automatically assume that others have negative intentions? Do you tend to make mountains out of molehills? Are you overly reactive and sensitive to what others say and do? If your answer to these questions is "yes," you are most likely the primary source of conflict in your life. Finally, people tend to engage in conflict when they are hungry, tired, or stressed. Know what causes you to "see red," acknowledge it, and give yourself some time to reflect and relax.

3. **Put things in perspective.** Figure out if an issue really exists or if you're being particularly sensitive due to your mood or other things that are happening in your life. Ask yourself if it is worth it to invest your energy in trying to resolve a particular misunderstanding or conflict (is the situation likely to reoccur? Is the issue important?). Appreciate that two people can have different perceptions of the same situation. Try to put yourself in the other person's shoes but don't take responsibility for how they feel. Don't project your own fears and weaknesses onto others. Don't make assumptions about the other person's motives and intentions. Ask yourself if this is a situation where you might "win the battle, but lose the war." For example, you might get your point across but you might tarnish your reputation and relationship in the process. Ask yourself: will this issue matter in 6 months? In a year? Is it a deal breaker?

4. **Ask yourself what the real underlying issues are beyond the obvious symptoms.** Sometimes, we tend to focus on what's happening rather than trying to understand why it's happening. Think about previous patterns of interaction that may have fueled the present conflict. Distinguish between facts and opinions. Try to restate the issues in a factual manner. Try to move away from personalizing a conflict and focus on specific issues or behaviors that are problematic.

5. **Try to resolve the issue directly with the other person** by using a win-win approach before involving others. Talk to the person directly and one-to-one. Avoid complaining to others (in other words, triangulation); instead of helping to solve the problem, this just spreads it around. Identify how you may have contributed in some way to the problem and accept responsibility for your part. Avoid being involved as a third party in someone else's conflict unless the people involved agree to have you serve as an intermediary, you have the skills to deal with the situation, and you feel like helping out. If all

three of these aren't present, don't intervene. Doing so will simply embroil you in someone else's conflict. Encourage people who have complaints about someone else to talk to that person directly. People who talk to you about others are usually quite willing to talk to others about you.

6. **Use your communication skills**: Demonstrate active listening: listen uncritically, don't overreact, be tentative, and take time. Respond to others' feelings. Don't agree or disagree, simply reflect their feelings. Summarize what you have heard and what you understand; draw on facts, feelings, and behaviors. Don't judge or accuse. This ensures that both of you understand what has occurred and keeps the line of communication open. Be assertive using the three Fs: state the **facts** of what happened, describe your **feelings** (the impact of what happened on you), and then explain what you want and need in the **future** in a non-threatening way. Don't make others responsible for your own feelings ("You make me feel …"). Attempts to make you feel guilty or inadequate won't work without your cooperation.

7. **Encourage two-way discussion.** Be prepared to "agree to disagree" if necessary. Focus on the problem, not the person and your dislike or disrespect for them. Obtain specific information: who, what, when, where, and how; and examples of specific behaviors and consequences. Try to appreciate the interests that are beneath the other person's position. Consider multiple alternatives for resolving the issue. If the other person tries to sidetrack you and change the subject, be persistent in communicating your message.

8. **Discuss options that both of you can live with.** Discuss goals that you can both agree on; for example, we both want the project to be successful. Say what you want in a non-threatening way. Move the conflict away from the past, where nothing can be changed, to the present and the future.

145

9. **Spend some time considering which approach is most appropriate** in the particular situation that you are facing and implement it. Don't feel that you have to agree to something on the spot. Ask for time to reflect.

10. **Ask yourself**: "What would (insert name of someone you admire) do in this situation?" Or, "What would a mature person who is able to exercise self-control and take personal responsibility do in this situation?"

Here is your challenge: Think of a conflict or misunderstanding that exists between you and another person. Using the 10 tips, try to solve the problem with the other person directly without the intervention of a third party. Focus on the problem and not on the personal characteristics that you don't like in the other person. Recognize your partial contribution to the problem and accept your responsibility in the conflict. Try to be sensitive to the other person's point of view. Find a win-win solution. Keep track of your efforts and results in your journal.

Reflection: Answer the following questions in your journal. How did you feel during this exercise? Was the conflict to be solved easy to identify? Were there others? Looking at 10 tips for constructive conflict management, which were especially challenging to follow? Easy? Why? What other strategies did you use that were helpful? How did your interaction go? What were the reactions of the other person? What lessons have you learned in doing this exercise?

Action plan: What five specific actions will you take starting now to (a) minimize conflicts and misunderstandings and (b) resolve them quickly and effectively? Keep a record of your plan and your progress in implementing your plan in your journal.

PART 4: TEAMING AND LEADING

18

ARE YOU IN OR ARE YOU OUT?

"Being ignored causes the same chemical reaction in the brain as experiencing a physical injury." – Kipling Williams

"There are many different kinds of death, not all of them physical. There are murders as subtle as a turned eye. Dante was inspired to install Satan in ice, cold indifference being so common a form of evil." – Anne Truitt

"For no matter what we achieve, if we don't spend the vast majority of our time with people we love and respect, we cannot possibly have a great life. But if we spend the vast majority of our time with people we love and respect – people we really enjoy being on the bus with and who will never disappoint us – then we will almost certainly have a great life, no matter where the bus goes. The people we interviewed from the good-to-great companies clearly loved what they did, largely because they loved who they did it with." – Jim Collins

"Make everyone a hero. Remembering to recognize, reward, and celebrate accomplishments is a critical leadership skill. And it is probably the most underutilized motivational tool in organizations. There is no limit to how much recognition you can provide, and it is often free." – Rosabeth Moss Kanter

In his classic book *Productive Workplaces*, organizational change specialist Marvin Weisbord says "each person in a work group continually struggles with three questions that are never answered 'once and for all.'" Here they are:

1. **"Am I in or am I out?** The more 'in' we feel, the better we cooperate. The more we feel 'out,' the more we withdraw, work alone, daydream, and defeat ourselves and other people."

2. **"Do I have any power and control?"** If you feel you have power and control, you will feel valuable to the team and on the lookout for your opportunities. You will feel like you have a say and can influence the decisions of the team. You will be more inclined to get involved knowing that your teammates will listen to you and will be open to your proposals, ideas, and initiatives. On the other hand, when faced with changes we can't influence, we feel impotent, and lose self-esteem. It doesn't matter how smart we are, how skilled, or how far up the ladder of success we have climbed.

3. **"Can I use, develop, and be appreciated for my skills and resources?** Tremendous skills, experience, and common sense exist in every workplace. What keeps us from tapping them are outdated assumptions about who can and should do what." If

you're able to use your skills to solve team problems, you'll feel valued and included.

Do these ring a bell for you? How would you answer these questions? If these questions resonated with you, it's because you understood their importance. People who are accepted and involved in the team tend to invest in it. These "in group" members develop a sense of belonging and feel accountable for the team's results. When people feel that they have a place in a team, they work toward achieving the team's goals. They put their skills at the disposal of the team and they cooperate with their teammates. In contrast, people who are part of the "out group" don't feel accepted or integrated into the team. They are more inclined to isolate themselves and do their own thing without worrying about others. They collaborate less because they feel that what they have to offer isn't valued.

According to psychologists Roy Baumeister and Mark Leary, **the need to belong is fundamental to human existence.** Their research emphasizes that a sense of belonging predicts physical, emotional and spiritual health, happiness, success, and even longevity. So when people are excluded from their work team, they are denied what is essential to life. Indeed, excluding someone, even if it is not intentional, may be a type of psychological violence. Moreover, the self-fulfilling prophecy may come into effect. The leader sees the in group members as being more involved and gives them more attention, support, resources, and responsibilities. As a result, their performance and confidence levels increase, all of which serves to confirm the leader's expectations of the employees. The opposite tends to be true for out group members. The leader may develop low expectations of them, offer them less support, less challenging work, and fewer resources. As a result, these employees may feel less motivated and less confident in their ability to do the work. This negatively affects their level of performance, which then confirms the leader's low expectations.

You may not be the leader of your team, but, as a team member, you share responsibility for its success. Is your team just a collection of individuals who do their work but never really interact with each other as a group? If so, keep in mind that a sense of team spirit or community is something that needs to be deliberately cultivated. It doesn't just happen on its own. Here are a few ideas for contributing to team spirit as a team player:

- **Try to include everyone in your in group.** Make a special effort to include all team members in what's happening. Don't ostracize or exclude others, and don't encourage others or simply stand by when others are doing so. Actively discourage the forming of subgroups and cliques. People may express their preferences for socializing with certain people during their own time, but they need to recognize that pursuing these preferential relationships in the workplace undermines teamwork. If you're the leader of the group, give all members the same access to yourself, feedback, resources, and developmental opportunities. Also, distribute work assignments in a way that is equitable and that permits mixing of employees.

- **Try to help others succeed.** Give credit where it's due; put others in the spotlight rather than yourself. This will nurture relationships and provide motivation to support you in the future.

- **Help others recognize their own importance**. Provide others with sufficient information, skills, responsibility, and authority so that they can grow to be autonomous workers. Celebrate successes!

- **Never hurt, demean, or be punitive toward people.** Show patience and politeness toward others who may not express themselves the same way that you do. Hurting people does not teach them a better way; it reduces their confidence and increases their view of themselves as failures. Here are some behaviors that might hurt or demean others:

o   Talking behind their backs.
o   Ridiculing them.
o   Discussing their inadequacies with others.
o   Paying no attention to them or their suggestions.
o   Berating them in front of others.
o   Punishing them with demeaning special assignments.
o   Encouraging them to try, then clobbering them when they fail.

- **Be sincerely interested in the people working with you.** Try to get to know other team members, and let them get to know you. Share your perspectives, and try to work well with others. Involve yourself with your teammates. Be willing to participate in team activities (on and off the job).

- **Don't worry if some conflict happens in your team**; it's normal. But, if conflict persists, this could derail your team. Try to address it directly, and work out some ground rules for how the team will function (define roles, responsibilities, accountabilities, and whatever else you need to get the team on track to success).

- **Do your share of the work (and maybe more).** Don't be a loafer who relies on others to pick up the slack for you. This breeds resentment and will catch up to you sooner or later. People get tired of hearing teammates' excuses and justifications for not carrying their weight. No one wants to have a reputation as a lazy slacker who does as little as possible.

- **Prepare for meetings, and go to meetings that are called** (and RSVP if you absolutely can't make it). Arrive on time, and be attentive. This isn't the time to take out your cellphones, Facebook page, newspaper, lunch, or nail clippers. Participate actively; be willing to contribute rather than relying on others to make the effort to take the lead. Try to find the middle ground when there are differing perspectives.

- **Cultivate the ability to work independently,** rather than being dependent on your supervisor for direction, guidance, and encouragement. Continuously develop and upgrade your skills and motivate yourself so that your supervisor can be confident delegating work to you (without having to remind you, watch you closely, etc.).

- **Take the blame for problems that you have contributed to, and find solutions.** Don't go looking around for others to blame or not admit to your errors. That's not productive.

- **Give everyone a voice in making decisions.** Don't insist on doing everything your way. Give people choices, especially in relation to implementing decisions. Let everyone have a say. Also, don't focus on the details to the exclusion of the bigger picture. See both the trees and the forest. Silence doesn't necessarily mean agreement. Maybe some people have just given up. Consider that, even if the outcome of a decision is great, if the process leading to the outcome was nasty, unfair, or biased, then people will question the outcome. Contrary to what Machiavelli might say, the ends do not justify the means. Evaluate the impact of team decisions on others; make sure that your rational decisions are also considerate of others. People have trouble buying into something that causes them to lose esteem, resources and relationships. Don't rush into making team decisions, but don't delay a decision unnecessarily. Find the middle ground that allows you to think through decisions while ensuring that they are timely.

Here is your challenge: Think about a team that you're a member of and answer the three questions presented at the beginning of this exercise ("Am I in?"). What makes you feel good about being a member of this team? Bad? How important is it to you that you're in the in group, that you feel a sense of power, and that your skills and knowledge are appreciated? Are there cliques or coalitions in your team? Are there people who seem to be left out of discussions, group activities, and other events? How are decisions made? With the help of your feedback team, brainstorm three sets of actions that you will take this week:

(a) To feel more included, valued, and influential on your team. For example, participate in team events, volunteer for challenging projects, and voice your opinions during meetings.

(b) To contribute to a positive team spirit. For example, send a message of congratulations to team members who successfully completed a project.

(c) To help a person who appears to be left out feel valued, included, and successful. For example, take time to get to know them, ask for their perspectives on a situation and how they're doing.

Implement these actions, and keep track of your efforts and results in your journal.

Reflection: Answer the following questions in your journal. What was most challenging about this exercise? What did you do? How successful were you? What were the reactions of others? What lessons have you learned in doing this exercise?

Action Plan: What five specific actions will you take starting now to: (a) feel included, valued, and influential on your team; (b) contribute to a positive team spirit; and (c) include and involve people who appear to be in the out-group? Keep a record of your plan and your progress in implementing your plan in your journal.

19

ARE YOU A GOOD FOLLOWER?

Would you say that you're a good follower? Would your supervisor agree with your assessment? Supervisors want employees who are dependable, loyal, and trustworthy. Some people see themselves as born leaders, and want to skip following others. They want to do their own thing, and they may have trouble taking directions and learning from others. But, as Tim Ferriss tells us, "When you are just starting out, we can be sure of a few fundamental realities: 1) You're not nearly as good or as important as you think you are; 2) you have an attitude that needs to be readjusted; 3) most of what you think you know ... is out of date or wrong." Tim Ferriss encourages employees, especially new employees, to follow directions, work hard, and be willing to do "dirty work" that others aren't willing to do. What do you think of his advice?

Barbara Kellerman from Harvard University identified five types of followers based on their level of engagement ranging from "feeling and doing absolutely nothing" to "being passionately committed and deeply involved." Isolates are detached, indifferent, and uninvolved; they go unnoticed, especially in large organizations. They're not aware of what's happening and they don't care about their supervisor. Next are bystanders who observe and are aware of what's happening but choose to not participate in it because it takes too much time, effort, or even risk to do so. "They may go along

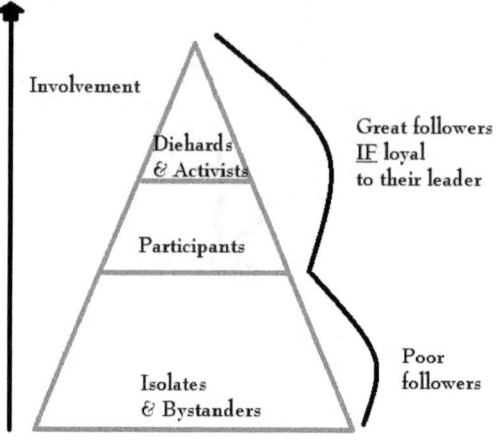

passively when it is in their self-interest to do so, but they aren't internally motivated to engage in an active way." Barbara Kellerman says that these two types are especially poor followers who tend to fly under the radar. In contrast, the remaining types are engaged in what's happening around them. Participants, for example, invest themselves and their time to influence what's happening. Activists are even more strongly engaged and invested in the team and are hard workers. At the very top of the commitment hierarchy are Diehards, rarely found, and "willing, by definition, to endanger their own health and welfare in the service of their cause." If they're loyal to their managers, they tend to be outstanding, sought-after employees who are in their manager's inner circle. But, if they don't support their supervisor, they cause problems. The key question is whether these followers are for or against their supervisor. What type of follower are you?

Here's your challenge: Think about a situation in which you're a follower (at work, school, or elsewhere). Reflect on your answers to the following questions and record them in your journal:

1. How well do you tend to follow your supervisor's instructions? (For example, if your supervisor asks you to outline solutions in your report, do you neglect to do so? Do you just do your own thing?)

2. Do you always meet deadlines? And do so without having to scramble at the last minute? (Or, do you like to think that you do your best work at the last minute or that deadlines are just guidelines?)

3. Do you work relatively independently and at a high standard so that your supervisor doesn't have to constantly follow up and assist you? (Or, do you do the minimum and only after constant prodding?)

4. What special efforts do you make to support and help your supervisors (including politely challenging them when necessary)? (Or, do you backbite, resist, and criticize them? Are you for or against them? They can tell!)

5. What do you do to get along well, collaborate, and build positive relationships with your supervisor and your teammates? (Do you wait for them to come to you? Do you minimize your efforts? Do you insist on getting your way or avoid others altogether? Do you take credit for their work?)

6. Are you engaged and willing to contribute to the success of the team? (Or, are you uninvolved, checking your cell phone, the clock, or your personal schedule during meetings?)

7. Do you tend to suggest new ideas for how to do things more effectively or efficiently? (Or, do you tend to complain about what you don't like?)

8. Do you tend to offer to do tasks that others find less desirable? (Or, do you cherry-pick what you volunteer to do?)

9. Are you enthusiastic and optimistic? What do you do to set a constructive example for others? (Or, are you grouchy or pessimistic? Are you the problem person?)

10. To what extent do you plan and organize your work and take initiative to figure out what's expected of you? Do you have a good work ethic? (Or, do you expect others to do all of this for you? Do you try to get away with doing as little work as possible?)

11. Do you try to learn in all circumstances? (Or, do you think that you have nothing left to learn?)

12. Are you hardworking and self-motivated? (Or, are you lazy, dependent, and need to be motivated by someone else?)

When answering these questions, rate yourself on a scale of 1 (never) to 10 (always), since things are rarely all or nothing. There may be some circumstances that influence your rating. Also, provide examples that support your rating. After you have answered these questions, ask your supervisor to answer them for you. Doing so will help you understand their perspective on your ability to follow their lead. Also, ask your supervisor what you can do to become an even better follower. Keep track of your answers and those of your supervisor in your journal.

Reflection: Answer the following questions in your journal. What do your answers and those of your supervisor say about you as a follower? In what ways were your responses to the questions different? Alike? What are your strengths and weaknesses as a follower? Which of Barbara Kellerman's five types of followers would you say you are? Why? If you were a leader, would you like to have a team of followers just like you? Why/why not? What lessons have you learned in doing this exercise?

Action plan: Starting now, what five things will you do to become a better follower? Take into account the ideas that your supervisor offered. Keep a record of your plan and your progress in implementing your plan in your journal.

20

WHAT KIND OF LEADER ARE YOU?

"Go to the people. Live with them. Learn from them. Love them. Start with what they know. Build with what they have. But with the best leaders, when the work is done, the task accomplished, the people will say 'We have done this ourselves.' ... To lead people, walk behind them." – Lao Tzu

"Become the kind of leader that people would follow voluntarily, even if you had no title or position." – Brian Tracy

How do you like your oatmeal? Hot? Cold? Not at all? Just as there was a perfectly warmed oatmeal and a comfortable bed for Goldilocks in *Goldilocks and the Three Bears*, so too is there a "just right" amount of leadership to offer to others. If we think of leadership as a combination of support and direction, leaders need to find just the right balance between these two behaviors. Too much support and encouragement can be

159

stifling, but not enough can be discouraging and demotivating. Likewise, too many directives and too much "telling people what to do" can feel belittling, but not enough direction and clarification of expectations can leave a person feeling lost.

Classic leadership approaches, such as Blake and Mouton's leadership grid, encourage leaders to offer up a mega serving of both support and direction to all team members. Leaders following this model believe that the best leaders are ultra-supportive and provide maximum guidance. They contrast this maxed-out style with three other styles: (a) the minimalist "leave 'em alone" delegating approach that offers next to no encouragement or direction to team members; (b) the country club "I'm here to support you" approach that emphasizes relationship-building at the expense of getting work done; and (c) the command-and-control model in which the leader doles out the work to be done along with precise instructions on how to do it.

The major problem with Blake and Mouton's approach is that each style is appropriate depending on the circumstances. If Bob simply delegated work to all his team members, some may not know what to do and some may not feel motivated to do the work. To extend the metaphor, the porridge may be too hot or too cold for some employees. Interestingly, younger and newer employees tend to use the maxed-out style because they are afraid of being seen as lacking in leadership if they don't provide a hefty serving of both direction and support. Unfortunately, when used in every circumstance, this approach is demotivating; employees feel like their leader is overbearing and in their face. So, contrary to Blake and Mouton's leadership grid, the maxed out style is not universally appropriate. And the command-and-control model is not much better. As leadership expert Jim Collins once said, "The moment you feel the need to tightly manage someone, you've made a hiring mistake. The best people don't need to be managed. Guided, taught, led – yes. But not tightly

160

managed." What to do?

Let's start by considering Dr. Glasser's view that we should never do for others what they can do for themselves. To do otherwise would be to infantilize them: telling them that we think they are incapable of doing something. It doesn't teach them how to do something or help them develop confidence in their own abilities. For example, if Coco always helped Bob solve his interpersonal problems, he would never learn how to solve those problems for himself. He wouldn't move from being dependent to independent (and, eventually, interdependent). She's not doing him a favor by constantly helping him out of jams. Now imagine if Coco were to start getting Bob to think through his problems, perhaps by asking questions about what he wants in the situation. This might give him a way of thinking about his problems that would enable him to resolve his own problems over time.

Ken Blanchard's situational leadership theory fits with Dr. Glasser's principle: leaders should offer as much support and direction as is needed by employees for a particular task. This means that leaders need to adapt their leadership style not only for each employee but also for each task. Sue might be super competent and motivated to perform Task A, but she might know nothing about performing Task B. When it comes to leadership, one size does not fit all! To apply the model, leaders need to follow this process:

1. **Identify the task to be performed.**
2. **Determine the employee's level of competence** (do they know what to do and how to do it; are they able to accomplish the task without direction or do they need constant feedback and guidance?) **and motivation** (how enthusiastic, committed, and eager are they; are they self-motivated or do they need the leader to be their cheerleader and active source of support?) **for this specific task.** According to situational leadership theory, there are four broad levels of development:

a. Level 1 – low competence, low motivation (high-need employees)

b. Level 2 – low competence, but motivated to do the work

c. Level 3 – competent, but not self- motivated

d. Level 4 – competent and self-motivated (ideal employees)

3. **Determine the style to adopt.** In keeping with the idea that you should only provide to your employees what they can't provide for themselves, an employee at level 1 should get the maximum dosage of both direction and support. Those at level 2 should get a lot of direction and guidance, but very little external encouragement (since they can provide this for themselves). Level 3 employees are the inverse of level 2 and should receive tons of support but little direction (since they know what to do, but they are discouraged in some way). Finally, the most developed employees, those at level 4, need very little direction and support; delegation is the appropriate style to use here. In contrast with the Blake and Mouton model, the situational leadership approach suggests that **the maxed-out style is only appropriate with high-need employees**. Ideal employees are both highly competent and self-motivated; for them, the maxed-out style would be excessive and discouraging. Delegating and letting go of any need you may have to intervene in their work and be constantly present, however difficult it may be for you, is essential for these folks.

A helpful way to imagine your employees' level of development is to consider that each of them has two elevators for each task – one for their level of self-motivation and one for their level of competence. When an employee is at the 4th floor of both elevators, they're able to motivate themselves fully without your having to encourage them, and they're so competent that they could teach others how to do the work. As you can imagine, you would want to simply delegate work to them, rather than closely

162

supervising or supporting them. However, if your employee is in the basement of both elevators, they are completely unmotivated and unable to do the task without constant supervision. You would need to try to provide a great deal of direction and encouragement to such employees. If your employee's self-motivation and competence elevators are in between, let's say at floor 2 for both, you would need to provide some direction and motivation, not too little, not too much. Ultimately, the goal is for employees to become more self-directed and reach floor 4 in both elevators.

At which floor is your self-motivation elevator?		At which floor is your competence elevator?
Super self-motivated! Offers support and encouragement to others.	4	Super competent. Can develop and direct the work of others.
Very self-motivated! No external motivation required.	3	Very competent. Can do the job without help.
Generally self-motivated. Requires external support and encouragement only occasionally.	2	Generally competent. Can do the job with very little help.
Somewhat self-motivated. Much support and encouragement needed, but not consistently.	1	Somewhat competent. Can perform the work with regular feedback.
Zero self-motivation! Depends on maximum and constant support and encouragement.	B	Zero competence. Depends on receiving lots of precise direction (how to do, what to do, etc.)

4. **Discuss with the employee the style you plan to use.** This allows you and the employee to discuss expectations and confirm your choice of style. This could also open up discussions that will improve the relationship as well as the satisfaction of both parties.

5. **Try to develop your employees by gradually decreasing your level of direction and support.** Hopefully, as a leader, you'll be helping your employees develop both their competence and self-motivation for all of their tasks so that they can become high functioning independent employees (level 4). How can you do this? First, you need to offer the right amount of leadership based on your team members' level of competence and motivation. Second, you need to move people along the developmental continuum: (a) give your team members increasing responsibility and independence as they become more competent; and (b) reduce the amount of encouragement and support that you offer as they become self-motivated.

6. **Intervene when you notice drops in either of these elevators.** Act immediately to support your employees by choosing a style that is similar to the style you are currently using (avoid changing your leadership style in a radical way) but that gives them more of what they seem to be lacking.

Knowing about leadership is important to you as an employee. It'll help you understand and influence how your supervisor is leading you. It will encourage you to develop your competence and self-motivation so that your leader can simply delegate work to you (which will provide you with more influence and autonomy). Also, knowing about leadership will help you to develop your own leadership skills. Sometimes as an employee, you need to help other employees do their work (when there are new employees or when you're the acting supervisor).

Here's your challenge: We all have preferences for how we are led and how we lead others. We tend to use the leadership approach or style that we prefer as team members. For example, if Sue prefers having a leader who primarily delegates work to her, trusting that she knows what to do and that she'll be able to motivate herself to do it, then Sue will tend to use this approach with her employees. In your journal, answer the following questions:

1. Which of these styles would you prefer your supervisor use with you? Why?
2. Which would you use when leading a team? Why?
3. How do these two leadership styles (your answers to #1 and #2) overlap?
4. How flexible do you think your leadership style is? In other words, if you had to rate your ability to adapt and shift your way of leading on a scale of 1 to 10, what score would you give yourself? Why?
5. How effective is your leadership style? In other words, to what extent (on a scale of 1 to 10) do you tend to choose the leadership style that fits best with your team members' level of development for a particular task?
6. How "developmental" are you as a leader? In other words, to what extent (on a scale of 1 to 10) do you try to grow your employee's level of competence and self-motivation? How well do you deal with challenges: when your employee is doing well and you need to reduce your involvement or when your employee's performance is dropping and you need to increase your involvement?
7. Now, looking at yourself as an employee, think about your three major job responsibilities and identify where your self-motivation and competence evaluators have stopped. What are you doing to improve your level of competence and self-

motivation so that your leader can apply a delegating style of leadership?

How often have you spoken with your supervisor about their leadership style? For example, when Coco's supervisor returned from a workshop on leadership, he started hanging around her office so much that it was getting in the way of her work. When she asked him about this, he said that he learned of the importance of MBWA – management by walking around – and being accessible, so that's what he was doing. He's an introvert, and he was told that introverts should stop using MBCD (management by concentrated desk time) and start doing what extraverts tend to do: MBWA. But Coco felt like he was babysitting her. He didn't realize that his MBWA was HHW (harming her work). She felt suffocated, and his presence was distracting her from her work. Coco felt like her supervisor didn't trust her to get her work done. She wanted him to manage by walking away! Finally, she took the initiative to have a discussion with him, and he agreed to return to his old way of managing: MBCD. Sometimes employees forget that they need to manage how they're managed. Awesome employees take initiative to clarify expectations and authority levels, keep their supervisors informed, negotiate resources and tools that they'll need to do a good job, etc. They don't just passively wait to be led. Awesome employees are proactive and positive in their interactions with their supervisor. And, they're easy to lead – they know what to do and can get things done without their supervisor's constant intervention or support.

Do you find it challenging to follow someone else's lead? As Rob Goffee and Gareth Jones suggest, we all like to say what's on our minds (some more than others). Sometimes we think that we're showing initiative by doing so. But are you able to hold back and resist sharing your opinion or doing exactly what you want when the situation calls for it? In an old song, Kenny Rogers sings,

"You've got to know when to hold 'em / Know when to fold 'em / Know when to walk away / And know when to run." In other words, you need to exercise some situational judgement. Sometimes, conforming is the best thing to do. Doing so, without compromising your values of course, might help you work more effectively with others and be more effective in the long run. Also, being open to others' ideas and being able to set aside your wishes for the time being shows humility.

Now that you've taken some time to apply the leadership model to yourself, your next step is to show your supervisor how the model works and discuss what you've written in response to the seven questions in your challenge. Be sure to schedule enough time to cover all the questions. Also, find out what your supervisor's perceptions are regarding:

1. The leadership styles they tend to use with you.
2. On which floors your self-motivation and competence evaluators have stopped for your three major job responsibilities.
3. What you need to do to improve your level of competence and self-motivation so that your elevators can move to the top floor.
4. What your strengths and weaknesses are in your ability to follow their lead. Do you disregard what they ask you to do and just do what you want, or do you pay attention to what is being asked of you?
5. Your approach to leading when you're called to do so (for example, when you're training new employees).
6. How flexible and effective your leadership style is (are you able to adapt your approach to the needs of others).
7. How "developmental" you are as a leader (do you try to help others increase their levels of competence and confidence).

Take note of your discussion and any agreements you make in your journal.

Reflection: Answer the following questions in your journal. Given your answers to the seven questions, what are the possible strengths and weaknesses of your leadership preferences – both how you are led and how you lead? What are some possible challenges that your leadership may present in the future? Explain how should the ideal leader "serve up" their leadership? How can employees help their leader choose a leadership style that fits with their level of development? How did your discussion with your supervisor go? How did your supervisor react to your answers to the seven questions? How did your supervisor answer the second set of questions? What agreements did you make?

Action Plan: What four specific actions will you take starting now to: (a) become more competent and self-motivated for your major responsibilities; (b) communicate with your supervisor about their leadership style; and (c) develop a leadership style that fits you and is appropriate to others? Keep a record of your plan and your progress in implementing your plan in your journal.

PART 5: MASTERING CHANGE

21

WHAT ARE YOUR TOP FIVE STRATEGIES FOR DEALING WITH STRESS?

"Adopting the right attitude can convert a negative stress into a positive one." – Hans Selye

"Every now and then go away, have a little relaxation, for when you come back to your work your judgment will be surer. Go some distance away because then the work appears smaller and more of it can be taken in at a glance and a lack of harmony and proportion is more readily seen." – Leonardo Da Vinci

On a scale of 1 to 10, how stressed do you generally feel? To what extent are you a source of stress for others? According to Richard Lazarus and Susan Folkman, stress is a "transaction between the person and the environment in which the situation is assessed by the individual as taxing his resources and potentially jeopardizing his well-being." That's why Coco and Bob, for example, can be in the same situation, but Coco feels stressed and Bob enjoys himself

170

thoroughly. Coco is experiencing a gap between the demands placed on her and her ability to cope with the demands. She needs to invest energy to cope with this gap, and she eventually feels strain. In the same situation, Bob feels able to handle the demands, and he may even see them as opportunities.

Dealing with stress is a natural part of an employee's job. P.D. Harms, a University of Alabama professor, and his colleagues analyzed the results of studies involving almost 50,000 employees from 25 countries and found that poorly coping with stress has nasty effects in the workplace. Employees who have trouble dealing with stress – and its long-term (chronic) counterpart, burnout – tend to have reduced job performance and satisfaction, more accidents and withdrawal, poorer decision making (especially when issues are complex), increased self-focus, a command-and-control style of working with others, and even increased aggressiveness and abusiveness. Moreover, stress is contagious. When people are stressed, they pass on this stress to others. These nasty effects of stress should be enough to motivate you to deal with stress effectively.

Although stress researchers used to focus on major life events as sources of stress, current research shows that daily hassles, micro stressors in our day-to-day lives, have a significant impact on overall stress levels. According to the extensive research of Anita DeLongis, Susan Folkman, and Richard Lazarus, small hassles encountered each day have an important influence on your health and your mood. Hassles are irritants, things that either annoy you or disturb you. They can upset you or cause anger and frustration.

However ordinary they may be, these stressors accumulate over time and hinder our wellbeing. The idea of daily hassles can be illustrated by an experiment involving a glass of water and 100 straight pins. When you place the pins in the glass of water one at a time and watch the water level, it's hard to notice any change. However, if you place all the pins in the glass of water at the same time, you'll easily see a change in the water level. Daily hassles are like putting one pin in your glass of water (your life) at a time. It's hard to appreciate their impact one at a time because it seems so miniscule. But the effects of their accumulation create significant stress.

It's the same with uplifts (things that make us feel good, peaceful, happy, or relaxed). You may not appreciate the impact of a smiling cashier, an elevator that opens just as you arrive, and the hundreds of other little pleasant things that happen throughout the day, but, together, their impact adds up. Recognizing uplifts is very important for awesome employees. For them, there is good in every situation, and they know how to appreciate it. As team members, they focus on each other's strengths, improvements, and successes. They limit the hassles so that everyone can feel good about contributing to the team.

You might find hassles and uplifts in your work life, your finances, your relations with family and friends, domestic arrangements, health, leisure or even in life in general. Depending on your experiences, you can even find hassles and uplifts in the same situations: workload, colleagues, customers, supervisors, the nature of your work, scheduling, organizing, paperwork, travel, weather, news, economy, government, your neighborhood, money, spouse, children, parents, your health, the health of family members, intimacy, family obligations, friends, your physical appearance, physical activity, medical care, free time, home entertainment, recreation, family time, meals, pets, cleaning, transportation, and more.

Because stress is contagious, you need to be extra vigilant when you feel the first signs of stress. This means identifying the daily hassles and uplifts in your life so that you can try to prevent the hassles and attract the uplifts. You also need to consider what works for you in coping with your feelings of stress. Although the best way of dealing with feelings of stress is to do something to address the situation directly, that isn't always possible. Stress is individualized; not everyone is stressed by the same things, and not everyone uses the same approach to coping with stress. This is why it's important to know yourself well enough to understand what triggers feelings of stress for you and what helps you deal with it.

Here's your three-part challenge: Part 1 will help you become more aware of your personal hassles and uplifts so that you can reduce the number of hassles that you face and increase the number of uplifts that you experience. For three days this week, before going to bed, prepare a list of all the hassles and uplifts you experienced during the day in your journal. Also, prepare a list of how you may have been a source of uplifts or hassles for others.

Part 2 will help you understand what stress means for you personally and what your best personal strategies are for dealing with it. This will allow you to: (a) understand what causes you to feel stressed (so that you can begin to minimize or eliminate these stressors); (b) quickly recognize the first signs of stress (so that you can deal with it right away); and (c) develop some personalized solutions for dealing with your feelings of stress. This readymade list of solutions will help you de-stress more quickly. In your journal, answer the following questions:

1. What are five frequent **sources** of stress for you? According to the Center for Human Stress Studies (CESH), feelings of reduced control and predictability, increased novelty, and a threatened ego especially in relation to workloads, finances, health, and relationships are likely to generate feelings of stress. Do any of these apply to you? If so, how? Some of the hassles that you identified in part one might be part of this list.

2. What are your early **signs** of stress? When you're experiencing stress, what are you feeling (e.g. anxious, sad, irritable, impulsive), thinking (e.g. negative attitudes, pessimism, reduced objectivity), and doing (e.g. isolating yourself, becoming aggressive, doing less work)? What are your physiological signs of stress (e.g. insomnia, decreased energy, headaches)?

3. What top five **strategies** or actions help you feel less stressed and more relaxed? These strategies usually fit in two categories: thoughts (how do I change how I think about it? e.g. problem solving, putting things in perspective, optimism, and gratitude) and actions (what can I do differently? e.g. talk with a friend, physical activity, meditation, deal with the problem directly). Even small things can make a difference in how you feel. Here are a few examples: taking a long walk by yourself or with a friend, reading an inspirational book, meditating, creating a list of things for which you're grateful, trying to solve the problem with a trusted friend, or going out for a quiet dinner.

In part 3, for the entire week, be attentive to your early signs of stress and modify the list you prepared in part 2 as needed. As soon as these early signs appear, use the strategies identified in part 2. Take note of the combination of strategies that works best for you. For example, going for a long walk and meditating may be the combination that best reduces your stress level. Evaluate the effectiveness of each strategy and their combinations in lowering your stress level. Remove the ineffective ones from your top 5 list of strategies and consider others that might be effective. Keep track of your efforts and results in your journal.

Reflection: Answer the following questions in your journal. What was your experience during this exercise? Were there any surprises? To what extent was your stress level reduced? What are your most common hassles and uplifts? What common themes were evident in your signs, sources, and strategies for reducing your experience of stress? Were your lists accurate, or did you need to modify them? What conclusions can you draw about your overall ability to reduce your feelings of stress? What lessons have you learned in doing this exercise?

Action Plan: What five actions will you take starting now to (a) lower the number of hassles and increase the number of uplifts in your life? In the lives of others? and (b) to better pinpoint your sources of stress and target your strategies for coping with stress? Keep a record of your plan and your progress in implementing your plan in your journal.

Food for thought:

☐ Don't get stressed out at the drop of a pin. Be cool, relax, and do what helps you deal with stress.

☐ Be present right now. Don't crowd your mind with thoughts of the past or the future. The past is gone, and the only way you can influence the future is through your actions right now.

☐ In any situation, try to be an uplift and not a hassle for others.

22

HOW RESILIENT ARE YOU?

"Character cannot be developed in ease and quiet. Only through experience of trial and suffering can the soul be strengthened, vision cleared, ambition inspired, and success achieved."
– Helen Keller

"People who are resilient display a great capacity to quickly regain equilibrium physiologically, psychologically, and in social relations following stressful events." – Alex Zautra

Expect the unexpected! Change is the only constant in life! When life hands you lemons, make lemonade! It's not what life throws at you that matters, it's how you deal with it! We've probably all heard these expressions. They suggest that, although change can be one of life's greatest stressors, it can also be a source of personal and professional renewal. They also imply that whether your life is in control or out of control is a personal choice. With the possible exception of ultra-glum folks who have sunk deeply into the "I'm not responsible" sinkhole of life, it's hard to argue with this optimistic, self-empowered, "it's up to me" perspective!

176

How long does it take you to recover from a stressful event? If you can "roll with the punches" and adapt to change and challenges successfully, then you probably have a high level of resilience. What helps you build your resilience? Janet Denhardt and Robert Denhardt suggest that resilient individuals make do with what's available (something they call bricolage). It's a process grown out of protective factors such as good coping skills, social support, emotional expressiveness, and interpersonal understanding.

We certainly wouldn't get any resistance from psychologists Suzanne Kobasa and Salvatore Maddi, who made a career of studying personal hardiness (a component of resilience, along with grit, resourcefulness, and mental toughness). Their interest in this topic was spawned through their research on the effects of change on the stress levels of managers who were experiencing a major corporate reorganization. These researchers found that, while half of these managers had suffered significant illness and chronic stress symptoms, the other half were doing great. The healthy and high performing managers had developed the four C's of hardiness:

1. **Commitment**: being involved and finding purpose; feeling deeply for themselves, for others, and for their work (versus alienation from others, work, and even life).
2. **Challenge**: feeling motivated to reach beyond their personal limits.
3. **Control**: feeling a sense of control over their immediate work, workload, and personal life (rather than helplessness).
4. **Connection**: feeling supported and involved with others.

Do you want to enhance your level of hardiness? Hardiness isn't something that just happens. Overcoming well-entrenched habits of feeling bored, powerless, and isolated requires deliberate attention and effort. It can be one of the most important things that you do for yourself.

Here's your two-part challenge: First, take a look at the four C's of hardiness table below and determine your level of hardiness.

High Level of Hardiness	Low Level of Hardiness
Commitment	
Have a mission Are actively involved in making it happen Overcome barriers	Bored Can't find meaning in things Can't find activities of interest to get involved in
Challenge	
See stressful events as positive, creative challenges See change as inevitable and welcome it as an opportunity to grow and learn	See stressful events as problems Feel threatened by change
Control	
Feel in control of your life Have a sense of personal power Look for ways to have more control in your activities Either take concrete action or choose to avoid getting upset about not being able to influence a situation	Feel powerless Are reactive in approaching to problems Are passive, let someone else solve your problems Get upset in situations where you feel little control
Connection	
Have a sense of support from and community with others	Feel socially isolated and lonely Feel alienated

Note your level of hardiness in your journal along with examples that justify your assessment. Next, think about how to get more of the four C's in your life at work and at home this week. Then, meet with your feedback team to brainstorm ways to help each other develop high levels of hardiness. Implement at least three of these ways of building hardiness. For a wealth of options and resources, you can do a quick Google search for psychologists Suzanne Kobasa and Salvatore Maddi and the word *hardiness*. Keep track of your efforts in your journal.

Second, this week, your challenge is to figure out how you can increase your ability to bounce back from defeats and difficult situations – and do it. When something unfortunate occurs, resilient people are able to recover quickly and adapt to changing circumstances. Part of developing your ability to bounce back in the face of adversity is developing confidence (I can handle it!) and optimism (It'll work out fine!) Both of these can help you handle challenging situations, persevere in achieving your goals, and make adjustments along the way when you experience setbacks. This part of the challenge is adapted from an exercise that Fred Luthans and his colleagues found to be effective in developing positive psychological capital, an element of which is resilience. Answer the following questions in your journal:

1. Think of a difficult situation in your personal or work life in which you feel stuck and unable to move forward. Describe what you have done so far and what you are thinking and feeling about the situation.

2. Describe what is under your personal control in the situation and what might be beyond your control.

3. Now, think about the aspects of the situation that you can control and brainstorm, in writing, all of the possible actions that you can take to help you deal with the challenging situation.

4. Finally, read your list and choose those actions that you commit to taking this week, and decide where, when, and how you'll take them. What are your next steps? What do you hope will happen? Once you've implemented your plan, reflect on how well it worked, and create a new plan if necessary.

Reflection: Answer the following questions in your journal. What was your experience during this exercise? Were there any surprises? How effective were your attempts to increase your level of hardiness (part 1)? Resilience (part 2)? What seemed to help and hinder you in this process? What lessons have you learned in doing this exercise?

Action plan: This challenge has allowed you to identify several ways to increase your hardiness and resilience in different contexts. What three actions will you take starting today to build your level of (a) hardiness and (b) resilience? Keep a record of your plan and your progress in implementing your plan in your journal.

23

ARE YOU A LIKE A BOILED FROG OR A TRAPPED MONKEY?

"The measure of intelligence is the ability to change."
– Albert Einstein

"You see what you are willing to see." – John Maxwell

"Despite my firm convictions, I have always been a man who tries to face facts, and to accept the reality of life as new experience and new knowledge unfolds it. I have always kept an open mind, which is necessary to the flexibility that must go hand in hand with every form of intelligent search for truth." – Malcolm X

Have you heard the fable of the boiled frog or the trapped monkey? Both point to the need to be flexible and aware of the ways in which we might get ourselves "stuck." Let's look at each separately.

Here's the fable of the boiled frog as told by Daniel Goleman: "Throw a frog in boiling water and it instinctively jumps out of the pot. But if you put a frog in a pot of cold water and gradually increase the  temperature, the frog doesn't notice the water getting warmer. The frog sits there until the water boils – along with the frog." Whether this fable is true or not, its central message is that it's easy to become complacent and let our routines and inertia gradually set in. The pattern only becomes visible when it is practically beyond our control. Perhaps, we ignore our bad habits or those of others. Or, we allow little issues to accumulate and, eventually, we see that we've created a big problem for ourselves by not addressing them. Another way of looking at this story is that sometimes change is introduced in an organization bit by bit and only in hindsight do we realize that a major change has taken place. This story also tells us that it's important to get the opinion of people who aren't "in the pot" with you such as your friends or your teammates. Sometimes, people looking from the outside in (outside "the system") are more objective and can more easily recognize dysfunctions and what needs to be improved.

For the fable of the monkey trap, we turn to *Zen and the Art of Motorcycle Maintenance*. In this book, Robert Pirsig shares the story of how locals decided to set a trap for monkeys who were stealing their food. Their trap consisted of a banana placed inside a hollowed-out coconut.

182

The opening of the coconut was large enough for a monkey to reach inside, but too small for the monkey to pull out a clenched fist containing the banana. If the monkey opens his fist, he can easily pull out his hand and run away to safety. But if he hangs on to the banana, he does so at the risk of being caught by the locals. His short-term goal (hang on to the banana) puts his long-term goal (be safe) at risk. It's his reluctance to let go of the banana that traps him.

Bananas are fixed ideas about how things should be. These may be ideas, principles, or ways of doing things that have worked well for you in the past. The problem is not the banana, as such, it's hanging on to the banana at all costs even when it doesn't make sense to do so. The problem is continuing to cling to these principles or methods as best practices, rather than asking yourself whether they are still effective. When we hang on tightly to our expectations, our ways of doing things, and our preferences, a certain rigidity sets in, and we become fragile and complacent.

Flexibility and adaptability are the calling cards of awesome employees. Awesome employees are open to questioning their preferred ways of doing things and are able to change their ways when the situation demands it. This ability to adapt and reinvent yourself is becoming especially important in our ever-changing world. Awesome employees are able to question, challenge, and shift paradigms (the accepted way of thinking about something), so that there's room for creativity. In contrast, people who doggedly hold on to their bananas or who ignore the fact that they're in hot water have preconceptions about what works and what doesn't work that blind them to new possibilities. They are stuck in a paradigm and can't envision how things might be different. They likely have a great need for control, a need to do things the same way they have always been done, and some concerns about letting go (equating it with failure, perhaps). It may be their ego telling them that they always have to be right, or they may have trouble coping with ambiguity. Either way, something blocks them and leads them to simply enjoy the warm water or hang onto tightly to their banana at their peril.

What can you do if you want to change your complacency, "stuck in the mud" behaviors, or rigidity? Here are three suggestions:

1. The first step to changing these behaviors and thoughts is to **realize that you're doing something that may need to be changed**. Observe yourself. Make a list of any routines and rules that you hold on to tightly and that tend to govern your life. Because you have blind spots, and you might not be aware of the ways in which you come across as particularly stubborn or routine-bound, it's important to ask others for feedback. They may see things that we don't see because we're very comfortably settled in the warm water (that is getting warmer). Sometimes, out of fear of giving us negative feedback, people may not share important information with us. Ask others to share specific examples of when you might appear to be rigid, stubborn, or stuck in your ways. Yes, this feedback might be hard to take, but it could be a game-changer for you.

2. Second, **reflect on these behaviors and thoughts.** Are they working for you? Are they keeping you trapped and constrained, creating problems with others at home or in your workplace, stopping you from finding solutions to problems, or preventing you from growing as a person? As part of this reflection, consider how stressed you are. Researchers have discovered that under extreme stress people tend to suffer from what is referred to as the *Einstellung* effect, a cognitive trap in which we rely on a mechanized way of dealing with situations even though more appropriate approaches may exist. It's the equivalent of hanging onto to the banana at all costs and not being able to shift your thinking. Imagine someone who has a hammer and applies it to all their construction projects, even though screwdrivers and planers may be needed.

3. Third, **plan some new actions and ways of thinking that will expand your universe**. Remember, just as it took time and repetition to create rigid thinking and behavior, it will take time and repetition to change it. You can't just stop your rigid thinking and behavior; they need to be replaced with more effective thinking and behavior. Try new things, and try to do things differently (even by a little bit). Stepping out of your routines and comfort zone will help you see the benefits of doing so. If your automatic reaction is to say "no" to invitations or new opportunities, take some time to evaluate why, and consider possible reasons for accepting these invitations. Do an experiment where you reverse roles with someone who has typically been the target of your rigid thinking and behavior; for example, let someone else dictate or decide exactly what you will be doing one evening, and see how it feels to be on the receiving end of that rigidity. If some aspects of your inflexibility are related to controlling how things are done in a situation, consider how you might get others to participate in these decisions. Compromising and being able to let go even a small amount might help you see the benefits of increasing your level of flexibility. Remember that wanting to always be in control is a sign of insecurity. Learn to release any bananas that aren't serving you.

Here's your three-part challenge: In **part 1**, over three days this week, pay attention to whether and how others might complacently comfort themselves in warm water, unaware of problems or issues, or rigidly hold on to their bananas (ways of thinking or doing things). Write examples of such behaviors in your journal.

In **part 2**, to determine if you're more like the boiled frog or the trapped monkey, or both, take a few minutes at the end of three consecutive days this week to reflect on your day. In your journal, answer the following questions:

1. Did you remain in a situation that was slowly damaging your morale? If so, what was it? What did you do or avoid doing?
2. Did you have trouble deviating from how you've always done things (leaping from a comfortable but potentially unhealthy situation into the unknown)? If so, what would you need to make the leap?
3. What ideas, expectations, or ways of doing things did you rigidly maintain without questioning their relevance or usefulness?
4. What ideas, expectations, or ways of doing things created stress for you or prevented you from making progress in your personal or work life?
5. In what ways did you challenge your established ways of doing or thinking about things?
6. Did you offer feedback to others as a way of giving them a hand out of the "boiling pot" or "monkey trap"? In other words, how did you serve as a person on the outside looking in for others or for your organization as a way of encouraging change? It takes courage to stick your neck out and talk about issues that others don't or won't acknowledge.

In **part 3**, identify and carry out three actions that you can take this week to step outside of the boiling pot and monkey trap (in other words, to increase your awareness and flexibility).

Reflection: Answer the following questions in your journal. This exercise demonstrates the importance of letting go, becoming aware of your blind spots, putting aside old ideas, being open-minded, and other attitudes and practices that keep you from moving forward. Was it easier to find examples of you or others behaving like boiled frogs or trapped monkeys? What recurring themes appear in your daily reflections? What were the primary ways in which you were acting like a boiled frog? What steps can you take to help others become aware of thoughts, behaviors, and circumstances that are damaging? What were your most impactful monkey traps? What are the potential disadvantages of these traps? What would be the long-term consequences if you continue to cling to these traps? What are other ways of thinking or seeing the situation that might help you get out of the trap, become more flexible and be more effective in the long term? What preventive measures did you take to ensure that you were aware of your situation, habits, and circumstances? What actions did you take to ensure that you do not fall into these traps? How effective were they?

Action Plan: What are the three most important actions you will take starting now to become less complacent or rigid and more flexible and open in your thoughts and behaviors? Indicate specific actions and timelines and how you will assess whether you have successfully completed your plan. Keep a record of your plan and your progress in implementing your plan in your journal.

Food for thought:

- Be flexible and adaptable in the face of change. The inconvenient truth is that sometimes the old way of doing things just doesn't work anymore. You have to venture out of your comfort zone and find new opportunities. That's how you grow as a person.

- Be aware of what is happening around you. Before you know it, a bunch of little changes add up to major change.

- Let go of any rigidities and things that are keeping you from progressing in your life. Hanging on to ideas that don't reflect reality is an exercise in futility and frustration. Don't stand in the way of change. Be part of it.

- "The hardest thing to open is a closed mind." – Ahmed Kathrada

PART 6: PULLING IT ALL TOGETHER

24

WOULD YOU HIRE YOURSELF?

"I hire people brighter than me and
then I get out of their way." – Lee Iacocca

"In determining the right people, the good-to-great companies
placed greater weight on character attributes than on specific
educational background, practical skills,
specialized knowledge, or work experience." – Jim Collins

"Somebody once said that in looking for people to hire, you look
for three qualities: integrity, intelligence, and energy. And if you
don't have the first, the other two will kill you. If you think about
it; it's true. If you hire somebody without [integrity], you really
want them to be dumb and lazy." – Warren Buffett

"If you can hire people whose passion intersects with the job, they
won't require any supervision at all. They will manage themselves
better than anyone could ever manage them. Their fire comes
from within, not from without. Their motivation is internal, not
external." – Stephen Covey

Would you hire yourself? Do you think that having great technical skills will make you a star candidate? Awesome employees have technical skills: they don't come to the party empty-handed, and they add value wherever they find themselves. However, they have more than technical skills. They are able to  manage themselves, work well with others, and show leadership, while at the same time being able to compromise and change.

Imagine that your dream position became available in your ideal organization, and you're on the short list for the position. Because of the high costs associated with hiring, orienting, and training employees and their potential impact on the organization, many organizations are being extra thorough in the selection process. They may ask candidates to complete psychometric assessments, participate in team simulations, and even go for lunch with potential coworkers. Your employment interview is likely to be structured and include a number of behavioral questions. Since the best predictor of future behavior is past behavior in similar circumstances, you'll likely be asked to describe how you have handled situations in the past. Well, today's your lucky day. If you have carried out the exercises in this book, you have lots of insight and experience to draw upon, and you should be able to ace the interview.

How might you answer the following questions?

1. What does being an awesome employee mean to you? Would you say that you're an awesome employee? Why or why not?
2. Tell us about your best and worst experiences as an employee and what you learned from them.
3. Tell us about yourself, your strengths and weaknesses, and what you've done to address your weaknesses.

4. Tell us about a time when you felt motivated. What about unmotivated? What did you do? What motivates you?

5. Share with us a time when you felt frustrated. How did you handle the situation?

6. Tell us what you have done to manage yourself effectively (your emotions, your attitudes, your behaviors, where you focus your time, etc.). Provide specific examples that best illustrate your points.

7. Describe how you went about setting priorities and getting your work done last week.

8. Tell us what you have done to develop and maintain effective interpersonal relationships. Provide specific examples that best illustrate your points.

9. Describe a recent conflict that you faced and what you did to resolve it.

10. Describe what you have done to generate and contribute to a sense of team spirit in your last team.

11. Tell us about your favorite and least favorite ways of being led by others.

12. Describe your personal leadership style and how you have applied it in your life.

13. What specific things have you done in the past three months to develop yourself?

14. Tell us about a time when you had trouble putting things in perspective. What did you do?

15. What specific actions did you take last week to deal with stress? Build resilience?

These are challenging questions and, of course, you are unlikely to be asked all 15 of them. However, it's a good idea to be prepared to answer them when the time comes.

Here's your challenge: In your journal, write your answers to any 10 of these questions. Be sure to provide anecdotes and examples that illustrate your points. Remember that you can find the "answers" in your journal. After you've written your answers to the questions, read them over looking for patterns and themes. Then, ask your feedback team to "interview" you and provide you with feedback on your answers.

Reflection: Answer the following questions in your journal. How did this exercise feel for you? Was it easy? Were there particular questions that were especially tough for you? If so, why? What patterns or themes emerged from your answers? What did you learn from the feedback team interview? What weaknesses should you address?

Action Plan: Describe three specific actions that you will take starting now to address the weaknesses uncovered while carrying out this exercise. Keep a record of your plan and your progress in implementing your plan in your journal.

25

WHAT ARE YOUR TOP 10 LESSONS?

"The ability to learn is the most important quality a leader can have." – Padmasree Warrior

10 lessons

Sometimes, the best way to appreciate how far you've travelled is to look back at the challenges and successes you've had along the way and reflect on what you've learned. Creating a synthesis of all that you have learned along your journey toward becoming an awesome employee will help you appreciate the investment that you've made in yourself and encourage you to continue to invest in your personal and professional development.

Here's your challenge: Identify and describe the top 10 lessons that you have learned in completing the exercises in this book. There are many ways to show what you've learned. An option is to read through your journal and highlight lessons that were particularly important to you. Then, look through your journal a second time, paying special attention to the highlighted text. Which lessons seem to reappear? Which are most important to you? Choose your top 10 lessons, and, for each lesson, complete the following steps:

1. **Name the lesson in one sentence in your own words.** Each lesson should be distinct. It should not simply repeat the contents of the book or be drawn directly from it.
2. **Describe the lesson.** What does your lesson mean precisely, for example, in relation to what awesome employees do?
3. **Describe why this is a significant lesson for you personally and how it represents new learning for you.** Usually, significant lessons are things we didn't know or do previously and that help us change what we think, feel, and do important ways. Describe why it's a striking lesson for you personally. If you have always known something, it's not a significant lesson!
4. **Describe in a concrete way what you will do differently in the future in the light of this lesson.** If this is a significant lesson, it must have important implications for your future behavior. It shouldn't make you simply continue what you have done in the past.

Use your creativity in developing and presenting what you have learned. By this point in your learning journey, your journal should be bursting with insights. If your journal is electronic, you can identify key words and phrases in your journal by creating a word cloud. A word cloud is an image or visual representation of the words in your document. Words that appear frequently in your document are presented in larger font sizes. All you need to do is enter your text in a word cloud website (such as www.wordle.net), and it will produce a word cloud for you. You can make adjustments for fonts, colors, and layouts.

Here's the word cloud for this book:

Share your 10 lessons and your word cloud with your feedback team, and get their interpretation and feedback. Include your 10 lessons, their descriptions, your word cloud, and your feedback team's interpretation in your journal.

Reflection: Answer the following questions in your journal. Was it hard to find significant lessons? How could you apply these lessons in your personal and work life? If you created one, how does your word cloud look? What did you find surprising or particularly interesting about your word cloud? How is it different from or similar to this book's word cloud? Describe what you have learned as you have progressed through this book by interpreting your word cloud.

Action plan: Describe three specific actions that you will take starting now as a result of the insights offered by your 10 lessons and your word cloud. Alternatively, you can create a 'to do' lists of things you will do and avoid for each lesson. Keep a record of your plan and your progress in implementing your plan in your journal.

REFERENCES

Baumeister, R. F., & Leary, M. R., (1995). The need to belong: Desire for interpersonal attachments as a fundamental human motivation. *Psychological Bulletin, 117*(3), 497-529.

Blake, R. R., Mouton, J. S., & Bidwell, A. C. (1962). Managerial grid. *Advanced Management-Office Executive, 1*(19), 12-15

Blanchard, K., & Hersey, P. (2008). Situational leadership. *Leadership Excellence, 25*(5), 19.

Burns, D. D. (2005). *Être bien dans sa peau.* Montréal, QC : Les éditions Héritage.

Cameron, K. S., & Quinn, R. E. (2005). *Diagnosing and changing organizational culture: Based on the competing values framework.* John Wiley & Sons.

Centre d'Études sur le stress humain (CESH) (no date). Recette du stress. Retrieved from: http://www.stresshumain.ca/le-stress/comprendre-son-stress/source-du-stress.html

Collins, J. (2001). *Good to Great: Why Some Companies Make the Leap… and Others Don't.* New York: Harper Collins.

DeLongis, A., Folkman, S., & Lazarus, R. (1988). The impact of daily stress on health and mood: Psychological social resources as mediators. *Journal of Personality and Social Psychology, 54,* 486–495.

Denhardt, J., & Denhardt, R. (2010). Building organizational resilience and adaptive management. *Handbook of Adult Resilience,* 333-349.

Dumont, M., Tarabulsy, G. M., Gagnon, J., Tessier, R., & Provost, M. (1998). Validation française d'un inventaire de micro-stresseurs de la vie quotidienne: combinaison du "Daily Hassles Scale" et du "Uplifts Scale". *International Journal of Psychology, 33*(1), 57-71.

Drucker, P.F. (2005). Managing oneself, *Harvard Business Review.* Retrieved from: https://hbr.org/2005/01/managing-oneself

Dyer, W. (1981). *The Sky's the Limit.* New York: Pocket Books.

Eddie, D. (2012, 11 octobre). What should I do about my bully brother-in-law? *The Globe and Mail.* Repéré à www.theglobeandmail.com/life/relationships/what-should-i-do-about-my-bully-brother-in-law/article4604565/

Einstellung Effect. (no date). Dans *Alleydog.com's online glossary.* Repéré à : http://www.alleydog.com/glossary/definition-cit.php?term=Einstellung Effect

Ferriss, T. (2017). *Tools of Titans.* New York: Houghton Mifflin Harcourt Publishing Company.

Frankl, V. (2006). *Man's Search for Meaning: An Introduction to Logotherapy,* Boston, MA: Beacon Press (Originally published in 1946).

George, B., Sims, P., McLean, A. N., & Mayer, D. (2007). Discovering your authentic leadership. *Harvard Business Review,* 85(2), 129-138. Retrieved from: hbr.org/2007/02/discovering-your-authentic-leadership.

George, J. M., & Bettenhausen, K. (1990). Understanding prosocial behavior, sales performance, and turnover: A group-level analysis in a service context. *Journal of Applied Psychology*, *75*(6), 698-709.

Glasser, W. (2010). *Choice Theory: A New Psychology of Personal Freedom*. New York: Harper Collins.

Goffee, R., & Jones, G. (2006). *Why Should Anyone be Led by You?* Boston, MA: Harvard Business School Press.

Goleman, D. (1997). *L'intelligence émotionnelle: comment transformer ses émotions en intelligence* (translate by Thierry Piélat), Paris: Robert Laffont.

Gottman, J. M., & Levenson, R. W. (2000). The timing of divorce: Predicting when a couple will divorce over a 14-year period. *Journal of Marriage and Family*, *62*(3), 737-745.

Hackman, J. R. & Oldham, G. R. (2005). How job characteristics theory happened. *The Oxford Handbook of Management Theory: The Process of Theory Development*, 151-170.

Harms, P. D., Credé, M., Tynan, M., Leon, M., & Jeung, W. (2016). Leadership and stress: A meta-analytic review. *The Leadership Quarterly*, *28*(1), 178-194.

Harvey, P., Stoner, J., Hochwarter, W., & Kacmar, C. (2007). Coping with abusive supervision: The neutralizing effects of ingratiation and positive affect on negative employee outcomes. *The Leadership Quarterly*, *18*(3), 264-280.

Jaffee, D., & Scott, C. (1984). *From Burnout to Balance: A Workbook for Peak Performance and Self-Renewal*, New York: McGraw-Hill.

John, O. P., & Srivastava, S. (1999). The Big Five trait taxonomy: History, measurement, and theoretical perspectives. *Handbook of Personality: Theory and Research*, *2*, 102-138.

Kellerman, B. (2007). What every leader needs to know about followers. *Harvard Business Review*, 85(12), 84-91.

Kobasa, S. C., Maddi, S. R., & Kahn, S. (1982). Hardiness and health: a prospective study. *Journal of Personality and Social Psychology, 42*(1), 168.

Kolb, D. (1984). *Experiential Learning: Experience as the Source of Learning and Development.* Englewood Cliffs, NJ: Prentice-Hall.

LaForce, T. (2017). 2 magic phrases to stop passive-aggressive behavior. Retrieved from: http://tomlaforce.com/2-magic-phrases-to-stop-passive-aggressive-behavior/

Lanctôt-Bédard, V. et Bouchard, J.-P. (2014, 6 décembre). *Quelques trucs pour améliorer votre écoute* [Online video]. Retrieved from: https://www.youtube.com/watch?v=5TI48GTK9VQ

Lankard, B. et al (1981). *Work Maturity Skills Instructor Guide.* Columbus, OH: National Center for Research in Vocational Education. Ohio State University. Retrieved from: www.eed.state.ak.us/tls/sped/SETforLife/VI_Work%20Experience/19WorkMaturitySkills.doc

Lazarus, R.S. & Folkman, S. (1984). *Stress, Appraisal, and Coping.* New York: Springer.

Luthans, F., Avey, J. B., & Patera, J. L. (2008). Experimental analysis of a web-based training intervention to develop positive psychological capital. *Academy of Management Learning & Education, 7*(2), 209-221.

Manz, C. C., & Sims, H. P. (1980). Self-management as a substitute for leadership: A social learning theory perspective. *Academy of Management Review, 5*(3), 361-367.

Maxwell, J. C. (1996). *Développez votre leadership.* St-Hubert, QC : Un monde différent.

McClelland, D. C. (1987). *Human Motivation.* New York: Cambridge University Press.

McKay, D. (1988). Depressed interactions. Presentation at the annual conference of the American Psychological Association.

Metcalfe, J., & W. Mischel (1999). A hot/coolsystem analysis of delay of gratification: Dynamics of willpower. *Psychological Review, 106*, 3–19.

Mischel, W. (2014). *The Marshmallow Test: Understanding Self-Control and How to Master it.* New York: Random House.

Ohno, T. (1988). *Toyota Production System: Beyond Large-Scale Production.* Danvers, MA: CRC Press.

Perkins, D. N. (2002). The engine of folly. 64-85. In Robert J. Sternberg (ed.) *Why smart people can be so stupid.* New Haven, CT: Yale University.

Pirsig, R. M. (1974). *Zen and the Art of Motorcycle Maintenance: An Inquiry into Values.* New York: William Monroe and Company.

Ravikant, N. (2017). Naval Ravikant on reading, happiness, systems for decision making, habits, honesty and more, [Audio]. Retrieved from: https://www.farnamstreetblog.com/2017/02/naval-ravikant-reading-decision-making/

Rodgers, C. (2010). Dix qualités recherchées des employeurs. Retrieved from:
affaires.lapresse.ca/cv/201001/19/01-940664-dix-qualites-recherchees-des-employeurs.php

Rousseau, P. (no date.). Droits et responsabilités. Retrieved from: http://www.bulletin-excell-pro.com/091-Droits_et_Responsabilites.html

Sherts, M. (2009). *Conscious Communication: How to Establish Healthy Relationships and Resolve Conflict Peacefully while Maintaining Independence.* Minneapolis, MN: Langdon Street Press.

Statton, J. (no date). What a goal really is and how you can get to yours [Billet de blogue]. Retrieved from: http://www.jeremystatton.com

Tolle, E. (2009). *Unité avec toute vie.* Outremont, QC: Ariane Édition.

Weisbord, M. R. (1987). *Productive Workplaces: Organizing for Dignity, Meaning and Community.* San Francisco, CA: Jossey-Bass.

Williams, J., & Babin, L. (2015). *Extreme Ownership: How U.S. Navy SEALs Lead and Win.* New York: St. Martin's Press.

Yokoyama, J., & Michelli, J. (2004). *When Fish Fly: Lessons for Creating a Vital and Energized Workplace from the World Famous Pike Place Fish Market.* New York: Hyperion.

Zak, P. J. (2008). The neurobiology of trust. *Scientific American, 298*(6), 88-95.

Zelenski, J. M., Santoro, M. S., & Whelan, D. C. (2012). Would introverts be better off if they acted more like extraverts? Exploring emotional and cognitive consequences of counterdispositional behavior. *Emotion, 12*(2), 290-303.

Zinger (no date). From *Merriam-Webster online dictionary.* Retrieved from: https://www.merriam-webster.com/dictionary/zinger

www.ingramcontent.com/pod-product-compliance
Lightning Source LLC
Chambersburg PA
CBHW071423170526
45165CB00001B/370